THE WALLACE

IN DEDICATION

Ni Challtuinn o' the grove,
Wi three times three,
Let this seed grow
Til a muckle tree.

DRAMATIS

MIRREN BRAIDFUTE, heiress of Lamington
JEAN, her servant
QUEEN MARGARET OF ENGLAND (French)
THE LADY ISABELLA, later Princess of Wales (French)
AILISH RAE

DONALD, a servant
SIR THOMAS BRAIDFUTE, Mirren's uncle
WILLIAM WALLACE
ANDREW MURRAY
SIR JOHN GRAHAM
SIR WILLIAM HESELRIG, English Sheriff of Lanark
MACDUFF, an older man
ROBERT BRUCE, EARL OF CARRICK
SANDIE FRASER, a spy
SIR JOHN COMYN, the " REID COMYN "
SIR JOHN STEWART OF BONKILL
SIR JOHN MENTEITH, his uncle
SIR JOHN SEGRAVE, English Governor of Scotland

PERSONAE

KING EDWARD I OF ENGLAND, aged sixty-five

THE EARL OF MARCH, "Blackbeard," Captain of Berwick Castle

THE EARL OF ANGUS

A MAJOR DOMO

SIR JOHN LOVELL, English Captain of Stirling Castle

EDWARD, PRINCE OF WALES

SIR WILLIAM OLIPHANT, Scottish Captain of Stirling

SIR RALPH HALIBURTON

AN ENGLISH HERALD

SIR PETER MALLORY, Justiciar of England

SIR RALPH DE SANDWICH, Constable of the Tower of London

SIR GEOFFREY DE HARTLEPOOL, Recorder of London

SCOTTISH CHRONICLER

ENGLISH CHRONICLER

Soldiers, Attendant Lords and Clerics, Ladies of the Court, Tumblers, Jugglers, Musicians, Pages, Trumpeters, and Artisans

ACTS

This edition of *The Wallace* has been reprinted to coincide with the 1985 Edinburgh International Festival production, in collaboration with the Scottish Theatre Company, performed in the Assembly Hall, directed by Tom Fleming and designed by Nadine Baylis.

The play was originally broadcast by the B.B.C. on 30 November 1959, produced by Finlay MacDonald. The first stage production was at the Edinburgh International Festival 22 August – 10 September 1960, in the Assembly Hall, directed by Peter Potter, with costumes and décor by Audrey Cruddas, and music by Iain Hamilton.

Deinde pedestrem Scotorum populum in prima acie collocavit, dicens eis, patria lingua, ita: " I have browghte ye to the ryng, hoppe yef ye kunne."

> [WALLACE, before Falkirk, as reported in the *Chronica* of William Rishanger, who died *c.* 1322]

The inscription on his tomb at Westminster Abbey—*Edwardus Primus Scotorum Malleus hic est. Pactum serva.*—commemorates his matchless activity, his determined honest nature.

> [R. B. MOWAT, *A New History of Great Britain,* 1926]

Could any Englishman doubt that justice was done, if brutally, when Wallace was executed?

> [From a leading article on the Nuremberg trials and executions, in the *Manchester Guardian,* 16 Oct. 1946]

ACT I

MIRREN BRAIDFUTE'S HOUSE
LANARK

May 1297

Some small magnificence, such as silver tassies, candelabra, etc.; a fine kist, a table on trestles, two or three wooden armchairs and stools; on the floor a large cowhide or bearskin.

Enter the SCOTS *and* ENGLISH CHRONICLERS, *carrying bread and wine, and followed by such* SERVITORS *as may be needful. Gravely, as in a ritual, and assisted by the* SERVITORS, *they set the scene, speaking their chronicles, between whiles, to the audience.*

SCOTS CHRONICLER

" When Alexander our King was deid, our gowd was cheyngit intil leid "; for then Scotland had nae prince and the great lords contendit for the Croun. It was a dour time for puir cottar folk. The great lords wished that Edward King of England should judge amang them wha should weir the Croun, and John Balliol was his man, and a puir man he was that the folk cried him Tuim Tabard, and Edward humbelt him and treatit him despitefullie, and it was a fell dour time for cottar folk, and there was nae peace in Scotland.

ENGLISH CHRONICLER

It was about this time that our good King Edward, hearing reports of the unsettled state of the Kingdom of Scotland, that was under his protection as overlord and superior, deemed it proper for the safety of that Kingdom that all castles and places of strength should be delivered up to him and that the Kingdom of Scotland should come under his dominion in the same manner as the Principality of Wales, for the preservation of peace in the Realm. And so he commanded his Justiciar in Scotland to outlaw without distinction all who refused to take the oath of fidelity, and these commands were diligently pursued.

SCOTS CHRONICLER

And sae, in the guise of friend and ally, Edward invadit and owrehailit the nation and did muckle skaith in slaughter and herschip, and wha wad nocht bow til his empire he gart be slain, and all places whar he passed he clean brunt, leaving nocht behint but stane and water. The great lords were aye at enmitie and made nae concurse, and Edward had his will in Scotland.

ENGLISH CHRONICLER

In the year of grace one thousand, two hundred and ninety-seven, out of their disobedience and malice, the perfidious race of the Scots began to rebel against the peace that the King had brought to the land. There was a certain bloody man, William Wallace, an outlaw, who called to his aid all who were outlawed like himself and acted as their chief and they increased rapidly in numbers and made great nuisance to the King's peace in Scotland.

SCOTS CHRONICLER

The month of May it was, in that same year, that William Wallace liftit up his heid. Inspyrit by God, he took pairt with the puir folk and wad deliver the realm. He had a leman, a noble leddie, that bade in Lanark toun and here [*setting candelabra on table*] he usit to visit privilie by nicht. It was in her house here at the Braidfute that all this tale began. . . .

Exeunt CHRONICLERS *and* SERVITORS.

Enter MIRREN BRAIDFUTE *and her servants,* JEAN *(carrying a basket of washing), and* DONALD. *It is dusk. As* JEAN *speaks,* DONALD *lights the candles.*

JEAN

Did ye hear the birds singin, my leddie?
It's a braw spring derkenin.
Simmer sune. Yon's a guid thocht.

MIRREN

Ay, and sae it is. God grant it bring
A spring til Scotland's fortunes, Jean.
Our winter's been owre lang.
What's yon? See gin it's them comin—

JEAN

No, my leddie ... Ay ... No, it's your uncle
Sir Tammas and twa o's laddies.

JEAN *runs to the entry. Enter* SIR THOMAS BRAIDFUTE *and two*
MEN.

MIRREN

Sae ye've come, Uncle Tam!

BRAIDFUTE

Mirren, my dear.

MIRREN

Come ben and set ye doun.
Donald, see to the lads.

DONALD

Ay, my leddie. Here y'are, lads.
There's yill ben.

Exeunt DONALD *and* MEN.

BRAIDFUTE

Are ye weill, lassie? Ye're lookin braw.
We've no seen ye doun in Kyle
For lang eneuch. It's no richt for a lassie
To byde here alane thir days.

MIRREN

But I'm no my lane all the time, Uncle Tam.

BRAIDFUTE

Ay, juist so. That fule man o' yours.
Is he here?

MIRREN

No yet. He will be, though.

BRAIDFUTE

He'll need to be quick about it.
It's gey near curfew.

MIRREN

Here, uncle, ye'll hae a tassie o' wine.
See to Sir Tammas, Jean.

BRAIDFUTE

Be thankit, Jean.

MIRREN

And dinna fash, Uncle Tam. He's a wyce lad.

BRAIDFUTE

He's a fule. And he's made you a fule.
The haill kintra kens o't. It's no richt,
Mirren. It's no decent for a leddie

4

O' faimilie, your mither and Hew
No cauld in the dust yet—

MIRREN

It is decent, nou, Uncle Tam.

BRAIDFUTE

Hou d'ye mean " nou "?

MIRREN

This forenune
We were mairrit here by Maister Blair—

BRAIDFUTE

Ye were what?

MIRREN

Mairrit, I said.

BRAIDFUTE

Without tellin me?   I had a richt,
Surelie, your legal guairdian—?

MIRREN

Ye'd hae juist forbad it.   Jean here
And Donald were witnesses.   [*Showing ring*]   See!

BRAIDFUTE

Weill, I'll be . . . !   No, I'll no—
I'll juist need to get used wi't.
But, och, lassie, my best brither's
Ae bairn, d'ye ken what ye've dune?
It was bad eneuch afore, but—
Och!   Nou, ye're tied wi this—

Frae this on, ye'll hae nae peace
Or chance of peace. Certies, ye'll hae
Nae husband, a huntit outlaw,
Landless, roofless—

MIRREN

Uncle Tam, can ye no see,
It's dune?   I've made my choice.
Words canna cheynge it nou.
My bairn'll be born in Cairtlin Wuids,
Maybe, but born in freedom—
Yon's mair—

BRAIDFUTE

Did ye say " bairn "?

MIRREN

I did.

BRAIDFUTE [*after a short pause*]

Ye mean ye're cairryin—?

MIRREN

Juist that.

BRAIDFUTE

Gin your mither
Was alive, she'd—your auntie'll
Certainlie hae a wheen words for ye
When I've tellt her.   Why did ye dae't—?

MIRREN [*laughing*]

Why did you?

BRAIDFUTE

Och, it's nae guid speakin—

MIRREN [*filling his tassie*]

Yon's better, Uncle Tam.

BRAIDFUTE

Be thankit, lassie.   I need it.
Sae this is why ye askit me up?

MIRREN

Is it no a guid why, uncle?

JEAN

—Here, he's comin, maistress!

Enter WILLIAM WALLACE, ANDREW MURRAY, *and* SIR JOHN
GRAHAM *with twelve men that gang round to the back of the house.*
GRAHAM *is gay, mercurial;* MURRAY *more serious.   All are young.*
They take off their swords and give them to DONALD, *who puts them*
away at the back. GRAHAM *kisses* JEAN *as he comes in.*

JEAN

Oh, sir!

MIRREN

Wallace!

WALLACE

Ah, my lassie! Ha, ha!—Sir Tam!
It's guid to see ye.   Are ye thinkin
O' jynin us, efter aa, then?
We've muckle need o' swords, Sir Tam.

BRAIDFUTE

Ye ken what I think, Wallace,
Weill eneuch—

7

MIRREN

        Jean, awa ben and help
Donald see to the lads.

JEAN

        Ay, my leddie.

                       Exit JEAN.

BRAIDFUTE [*to* GRAHAM *and* MURRAY]

Guid e'en til ye, sirs.

        Curfew tolls.

Ye cut it fine the nicht, though.

GRAHAM

We dinna heed the curfew muckle, Sir Tam.

WALLACE

Sir Tam, ye ken Andra Murray?
Sir Tammas Braidfute, Andra.

MURRAY [*with a bow*]

Sir Tammas.

BRAIDFUTE

     Sir.

WALLACE

        Ah, Sir Tam, I'm glaid
Ye're here to celebrate.   Has Mirren
Tellt ye?

BRAIDFUTE

     Has she tellt me?
Byde you till I tell you what—

8

WALLACE

Sir Tammas, no! This isna the moment.
We'll hear syne all ye hae to say—
But nou, we maun drink to fortune!
Dae your dutie, lass!

MIRREN *serves wine.*

Andra! John!
Drink our healths, Mirren and me!

GRAHAM

Ah, man, will we no dae juist that!

MURRAY

Guid health t'ye baith!

BRAIDFUTE

Ay, ay, indeed!

They drink

WALLACE

And nou—to Scotland!
To Mirren and Scotland!

GRAHAM

And daith to the Sudron!

They drink.

BRAIDFUTE

To peace!

WALLACE

Ach, Sir Tam,
Ye're no on yon auld tack again.

BRAIDFUTE

It's the ae tack can save Scotland
Frae bleedin til daith, Wallace,
And when ye're aulder, ye'll understand—
Gin ye live lang eneuch—

MURRAY [*quickly changing the subject*]
Hou are things wi you in Kyle, Sir Tammas?

BRAIDFUTE

Ach, bad, Murray, gey bad.
The folk are sair doun-hauden,
And, as I've tellt the Governor at Ayr,
Gin he doesna ease things, he'll hae
Reid rebellion on his hands
—Juist mair bluid to feed our barren land,
The ae nouriture she gets thir days,
Scots and English baith; and nae problem
Richtit at the end o't.

GRAHAM

It'll mean
Bluid aaricht.   And nae problem
Richtit wiout the sheddin o't.

BRAIDFUTE

I dinna haud wi yon kin o' talk,
As ye ken—but I canna blame young lads—
The liberties Percy gies his troops,
Ye wadna believe. . . .

GRAHAM

By the Rood, they'll rue it!
Why're we idle?

WALLACE

We want numbers.

MURRAY

Gif but the lords gae a lead!
Gin they had the luve o' Scotland
They hae for their ain acres. . . .

WALLACE

They canna think yon gait, Andra.
Scotland for the lords is monie
Lordships, no a folk. And the folk,
Wantin chiefs, murmur, but winna muve—

GRAHAM

We maun muve them!

BRAIDFUTE

Na, na, na, na! *Na,* Graham!
Yon's no the road at all—

WALLACE

The time'll come, John.

BRAIDFUTE

Listen to me—!

Enter JEAN.

MURRAY

Och, sirs, sirs, this is no the time
Or place for politics, at a waddin-feast.
This is Leddie Mirren's bridal!
Fill up the tassies, sirs, and be mirrie!

Andra, ye're the wyce man!
Uncle Tammas! Will! Sir John!

JEAN *pours drinks.*

BRAIDFUTE

Be thankit, lassie. Nou, hear me—

MURRAY

Sir Tammas, I pray ye—

BRAIDFUTE

No, this maun be said! Wallace,
Ye shouldna dune this to Mirren.

MIRREN [*with a laugh*]

It taks twa, uncle—

GRAHAM

Ay, juist!

BRAIDFUTE

No: ye shouldna be in the house,
In Lanark, even, the day—

WALLACE

Ach, Sir Tam!

BRAIDFUTE

I tell ye, Heselrig's dementit.
He's sworn to kep ye. Wi this
Curfew, his patrols gang round
Ilka house to check aabodie's in.
They'll be here the nicht. It's

No fair to Mirren. She's your wife,
Nou, and my cause baulder for it.
Isna your dutie first to her
In the haill world? Mak your peace
Wi the Sheriff as I hae dune,
As your ain Uncle Richard has dune—

GRAHAM *and* MURRAY *laugh loudly.*

WALLACE

The Sheriff? The anelie peace
Heselrig will get frae me's a lang
Sleep at the end o' a lang sword. Ha! Ha!

JEAN

My leddie, should ye no—?

MIRREN

No, Jean.

BRAIDFUTE

It's nae lauchin maitter. I mean it.
This, Wallace lad, is your chance.
Mak your peace wi honour—

WALLACE

Honour?

BRAIDFUTE

Ay, honour. Gin ye dae homage
Til King Edward, ye'll get pairdon,
And ye'll get back your land. For the sake
O' your faimilie, for the sake
O' Mirren, for the sake o' Scotland.
Peace will get peace, as bluid bluid.

Ach, Sir Tammas, I ken your hairt speaks.
Hou can I tell ye? Will ye never
Understand, this Edward, this blousterin
Tyrant, can hae nae peace in Scotland
Ever? The ae peace he kens is slaverie.
I'll dae homage til King John Balliol,
Richtfu King o' Scots, and til nae ither king.
There can be nae King Edward
In Scotland wi honour. Ever!

GRAHAM

Never! Yon's the word! Come, drink
To yon, at least, Sir Tam—

MURRAY

     Ay, ay, John,
While there's three o's alive!

They drink.

JEAN [*apart*]

My leddie—tell!

MIRREN

Jean, haud your peace!
I'll tell when it's time to tell.

BRAIDFUTE

There's owre monie tosts being drunk
For guid counsel nou, I'm thinkin.
Tell me, lad, hou's aa wi ye in the wuids?
Dinna tell me whar—I dinna wish
To ken.

Ach, we're gaun on, Sir Tam.
Cairtlin Wuids is muckle eneuch
To get lost in.   And we're no that idle,
For aa the Graham says.   No a day
Sees our blades unbluidie.   We're learnin
The tred o' war by scrimmage.
We canna tak the field; we strike
Like wolves, nou here, nou there, by nicht,
Frae ambusk, whiles by day as weill.
They hae nae rest, can ne'er be sure
What day will bring.   And aa the time
We learn.   Sune we'll hae an airmie
And then, Sir Tam, ye'll see—

JEAN

My leddie, d'ye no think—?

MIRREN

Jean, be still, will ye?
It's for me to say—

WALLACE

What's aa this, lassies?

MIRREN

Ach weill—Wallace, ye maun ken this—
I couldna tell ye—I'm sae blyth the nicht—
Ah, Will! but the time's come, ay Jean—
The blythsome bridal's endit owre sune—

WALLACE

What is aa this, Mirren?

MIRREN

Wallace, Heselrig was here—

WALLACE

What?

MIRREN

Efter you left wi Maister Blair—

WALLACE

Mirren, tell me—

MIRREN

He'd heard ye were in Lanark—

JEAN

He kent ye were mairrit the day, sir—

MIRREN

Hou could he, Jean?

JEAN

He kent. I'm shair he kent.
Yon's what brocht him here.
I'm shair o't—

WALLACE

What happen't, Mirren?

MIRREN

As Uncle Tam said; he's sworn to kep ye,
Will. Yon fray at the kirk on Sunday's
Put him daft—He's efter ye—

WALLACE

I've nae dout o' yon! What, then?

MIRREN

He spierit at me whar ye were, juist—

JEAN

Ay, and spier't at mair nor yon, tae—!

WALLACE

Mirren!

MIRREN

Ah, Wallace,
It puts shame on me to think on't.
I dinna wish to—here—

WALLACE

Did he touch ye?
Did he lay a finger on ye?

MIRREN *bows her head.*

JEAN

He wad hae my leddie gang wi'm
Til the Castle, sir; and—

MIRREN

Be still, Jean. Or gang!

WALLACE

Weill . . . ?

JEAN

I'll gang,
But I'll tell, my leddie, gin you canna.
It's for the best I tell. Sir,
He threaten't my leddie—
He put his airm about her—

WALLACE

Slave!

He starts, looks for his sword and buckles it on while speaking.

Nae mair? He didna force ye?
Speak, Mirren, did he force ye?

MIRREN [*shaking head and sobbing*]

No, Will, he didna.
He said he could byde for his answer.
He'd be back. He didna mean what
Ye're thinkin, I'm sure, but—
I was feart. I was gaun to tell ye
When we were our lane the nicht.
But we'll be awa the morn's morn,
Awa til the wuids and freedom
O' sic shame and pultriness.

WALLACE

Ay, we'll be awa aaricht. And, ay, he'll
Byde aaricht, but for me, and it's I sall
Be back, sir knicht; Heselrig
Will never see thy face again—
Or onie face but his Makker's.

MIRREN

Oh, no! Dinna lea me, Will!

WALLACE

Graham, get the lads in the street!
Tell them to be quaet.   Surprise
Is the shairpest sword.   We'll lea the horses
And get them on the road back.

GRAHAM

Ay, Will; guid!

Exit GRAHAM.

WALLACE

I'll be back,
Mirren, dinna fash! But first—

MIRREN

Will, please me and dinna gang!

WALLACE

Peugh! What d'ye think o' me, woman?

BRAIDFUTE

Wallace, ye're to byde here!
Ye'll dae nocht to danger my niece
Mair nor ye've dune or this
Wi your stramash and your discord.

WALLACE

Sir Tammas, ye're auld, and your bluid
May be thin, but ye spak til me,
The nicht, o' honour! I'd hae ye mynd
O' yon. As ye like yon brock Heselrig
Sae weill, get doun on your hunkers
And pray for his soul. Sair he'll need it,
Man, for this is Heselrig's
Last nicht on earth.

Clatter of armed men gathering, off. Torches, voices. Re-enter
GRAHAM *with* DONALD.

GRAHAM

I tellt Donald he couldna come wi's.

WALLACE

Ay, John. Ye're needit here, Donald.
Guaird your leddie weill. Come on, lads.

Will, please! No the nicht! Juist
No the nicht. I'm feart, Will.
On my bridal, the ae nicht
Of aa my life for this to hap!
It's my richt, Will, the richt
O' onie woman, surelie. Ah, Will!

WALLACE

We're aa readied?

GRAHAM

Ay, Wallace.
I tellt the men why and their teeth shut.
They've bluid in their een, the nicht.

BRAIDFUTE

Wallace, as Mirren's tutor I forbid ye!
This is wicked vain follie and ye ken it—

WALLACE

Ach, haud your peace, auld carle!
There's man's work to be dune.
Say your prayers!

He embraces MIRREN *close.*

Mirren, luve,
I'll be back sune . . . juist byde a wee. . . .

MIRREN

Byde? Byde? Oh, Will, I'll byde
Till daith! But byde ye, byde ye
This ae nicht. Murray, tell him!

MURRAY

I canna, Leddie Mirren.

I'll be back, luve. Come on, Murray!
Donald, bar the door and open til naebodie
But us. The word is " Ellerslie."
Nou, the lave o' ye, gang aa til your beds.

He kisses MIRREN.

Nae lichts. Come on, Graham.

Exeunt WALLACE, MURRAY, GRAHAM.

MIRREN

Wallace! Fare weill!

MIRREN *greits, comforted by* JEAN. BRAIDFUTE *pours a drink for himself and pats her on the back.* DONALD *bars the door and snuffs candles, but one or two for a dim licht. A slow scene, till* HESELRIG'S *entrance.*

JEAN

Wheesht, my leddie, wheesht! He'll be back.

MIRREN

No, no. I ken it. He's gane, Jean!
I'll never see him mair, I ken.
Oh, Uncle Tam, pray as he said—
But pray for Wallace my beluvit.
Why did ye no haud him frae gaun? They'll
Kill him. Och, I'm feart, I'm feart the nicht.

BRAIDFUTE

There nou, lassie, dinna greit.
He's a stairk bauld lad, and he's
No his lane. And the English'll
All be in the Castle lang or this—

MIRREN

But the patrol—!

21

BRAIDFUTE

There's but a dozen men in the curfew
Patrol. Wallace'll sort them eithlie.
He and Graham and Murray alane
Could deal wi a score. Hae nae fear, hen.
Thy lad'll be back sune eneuch,
And the morn ye'll be awa.

MIRREN

Ay, we'll be awa the morn's mornin.
Yon's a guid thocht.

BRAIDFUTE

It's better sae.
Though I canna like the thocht o' sic
A life for ye, but maybe's better sae.
Here, drink this, lass, and syne t'your bed.

MIRREN

Oh, no, I'll no can sleep while Wallace
Raids in Lanark streets. Ay, be thankit,
Uncle Tam.
She drinks.

But nae sleep
For Mirren Wallace the nicht. I'll onwait
His gain-comin.

JEAN

Ye'd be mair cosh
In your bed, my leddie. Come tae bed, nou.

English voices, torches, clatter, off.

MIRREN

What's yon? Are they back sae sune?

22

ENGLISH VOICE [*off*]

Halt! Surround the house!
You six at the back. Six with me.

BRAIDFUTE

Thae's nae Scottish men!

Hammering at door.

ENGLISH VOICE [*off*]

Open in the name of the King!

MIRREN

It's the patrol!

DONALD

Shall I open, Sir Tammas?

MIRREN

No, Donald. Wallace said anerlie til him.

Hammering.

ENGLISH VOICE

Open this door! In the name of the King.

BRAIDFUTE

Ye'd better, Donald. They'll juist
Brust in onieways.

ENGLISH VOICE

Open!

Hammering.

DONALD [*letting them in*]

Ye're a gey noisie lot, shairlie.

Enter SIR WILLIAM HESELRIG, *Sheriff of Lanark, and six* TROOPERS.

HESELRIG

Two of you on the door.—Good evening,
Mistress Braidfute. Pardon my want
Of ceremony, but we are in a hurry.
You are very dark in here.

MIRREN

We were gaun to bed. Lichts, Donald.
Will ye tak some wine, Sheriff?

HESELRIG

Thank you, my lady. A double pleasure
From your hand.

MIRREN

Jean,
Some wine for the Shirra.

HESELRIG

Hm! And may I have the pleasure
Of meeting this gentleman?
Two of you guard him, and two the churl.

MIRREN

Sir Tammas Braidfute, my uncle.
Sir William Heselrig, Sheriff
Of Lanark, Uncle Tam.

DONALD *lights candles.*

BRAIDFUTE

We are acquaint.

HESELRIG

Of course, of course.
I did not recognise you in the darkness,
Sir Thomas.   Your servant.

BRAIDFUTE

Your bird has fleed.

HESELRIG

Indeed?   What bird, Sir Thomas?

Silence.

A dour Scot, eh?   But I will guess.
Mistress Braidfute, you and I were talking
Of him only this afternoon, were we not?
Let us resume, shall we?   Tell me, madam,
Have you seen aught of our friend the outlaw,
The murderer, the rebel and traitor,
Tonight?
Silence.

You are all very silent. . . .

MIRREN

I dinna recognise in your description
Onie I'm acquaint wi, Sir William.

HESELRIG

Really.   And Sir Thomas?   My visit
Seems to have taken you all a little
By surprise.   I wonder why.
To be sure, the Sheriff of Lanark
Does not often command a curfew patrol
Personally;   but tonight I felt
Like fresh air.   It is a fine spring night.

Also, I must confess, I had hoped
To meet the outlaw Wallace here.
He was here earlier, was he not?

Pause.

Well, he was.   I know perfectly well he was.
This is a very pleasant wine,
Mistress Braidfute—or Wallace,
Should I say?   There are rumours.   Ah, well.
I must get some for myself, and you
Must come and help me drink it—what
Do you say?   But to business.
Where is Wallace, madam?

Pause.

When did you
See him last?

Pause.

Where does he hide
When he is not here?

Pause.

MIRREN

I hae nae answers for ye, Sheriff.

HESELRIG

I think you have, madam.

MIRREN

Then ye maun think again, Sheriff.

HESELRIG

Why so?   I am not your enemy.
Indeed, as you know, I am your admirer.

Who would not be? Wallace need not
Be my enemy either. I merely
Wish to persuade him to a wiser course
Than he is pursuing. Wiser for him
And for you and for us all. And you
Can help me, madam, and so help yourselves—

What wey div ye taunt a defenceless
Woman, Sir William? I can tell ye
Nocht and gie ye nocht.

HESELRIG

But you can. You have given me
Some excellent wine, and you can bring me
To Wallace, or—Wallace to me.
This is folly—is it not, Sir Thomas?
What chance has Wallace against
The might of King Edward? One day
We shall take him, surely. It is but
A matter of time—what of your lover,
Then, my dear, hanging from a tree
For the crows to kiss?

MIRREN

Ye'll never—

HESELRIG

You can prevent all that.
You can save him, Lady Mirren.
Come with me to the Castle, as my *guest*—
For his sake. He will surely follow.
You will be quite safe in my protection.
And so will he. I wish only to speak
With him—an innocent stratagem

To save a life, surely.   And we could
Be merry, could we not, my lady,
Awaiting him?   Some wine, some music?

MIRREN [*bursts out sobbing*]

Why div ye speak like this to me,
Shirra?   It's no richt!

BRAIDFUTE

Desist, Heselrig!   This is nocht
In your commission—!

HESELRIG [*striking him*]

Silence, Scot!   You speak when spoken to.
You are very stubborn, my dear,
And very foolish.   Now listen.
I have offered you the way of conciliation,
Of, shall we say, combination—
But I can use force, madam, and I will,
I promise you.   I want Wallace,
And I shall get Wallace.
This very night I shall take you
With me to the Castle—

MIRREN *gasps*.

JEAN

Oh, my leddie!

BRAIDFUTE [*starting up*]
              Heselrig, hae dune!
What skelartrie is this?   Are men
Sae scant that ye maun herrie
Lasses for your King?   I bid ye
Desist, or answer for't in bluid!

BRAIDFUTE *draws his sword but* TROOPERS *grip him*.

Lowse me, villains! Gar them tak
Their clairtie hands—

On the contrary, Sir Thomas, they have
Acted quite correctly. If, however,
You will promise not to interrupt
My conversation further with your
Childish taunts, you may sit down
Freely. Have I your word?

BRAIDFUTE

Ye hae nocht!

HESELRIG

As you will.
To continue, madam. This very night;
Now, in fact. That is a promise. Unless. . . ,

MIRREN

Never, never, never!
Ye'll kill me first!

HESELRIG

We shall see.
But you have not heard my condition—
And I promise you I am a man of my word—
I shall take you [*slowly*] to Lanark Castle tonight,
As my *prisoner*, unless you answer
My questions truthfully. You know them
Well enough. Where is Wallace? When did you
See him last? Where does he skulk
When he is not here?

BRAIDFUTE

Tell him,
Mirren. Wallace'll win awa.

MIRREN

I canna tell ye.

HESELRIG

Very well.

BRAIDFUTE

I'll tell ye, filth, gin ye let her be.

HESELRIG [*striking him on the other cheek*]

Your fate is already written,
Clown. Tell me!

BRAIDFUTE

D'ye sweir,
On your aith as a knicht, that ye'll molest
The Leddie Braidfute nae further
Gin 1 tell ye?

HESELRIG

I do.

BRAIDFUTE

D'ye promise?

HESELRIG

I promise.

MIRREN

Dinna tell, Uncle Tam, dinna tell!
Let me dee, but dinna tell!

I am waiting.

BRAIDFUTE

He was here the nicht.

HESELRIG

As I thought.
Where is he now, informer?

BRAIDFUTE

Words frae the like o' you canna
Hurt me, Shirra. Sauf them to fyle
Your parritch. Wallace is in Lanark.

HESELRIG

The devil, no! You lie, wretch!
How could I have missed him?

MIRREN

Ye'll aye miss him. My Wallace'll
Ne'er be taen by a Sudron—

HESELRIG

He will not be " your " Wallace
For long, my dear, if your uncle
Does not hurry with the final
Question. Where does he hide?

BRAIDFUTE

That I canna tell ye. I dinna
Ken mysel.

HESELRIG

You lie again, dog!
Unless you tell me, I am relieved
Of my bargain—and your niece comes with me. . . .

BRAIDFUTE

I canna tell ye what I dinna ken.
Yon's the truth.   Naebodie but his ain
Men kens his bield.   Certies, I dinna.

HESELRIG

You admit he was here tonight.
I would remind you that sheltering
An outlaw and traitor is a capital crime.

MIRREN

Wallace is nae traitor!

HESELRIG

He is a traitor to King Edward.

BRAIDFUTE

He was never liege o' King Edward's.

MIRREN

Neither ever will be.

HESELRIG

It would be the wiser course, all the same.
But your case is somewhat different,
Sir Thomas Braidfute.   You are
Liegeman to the King.   If you withhold
Information of a traitor, you too
Are a traitor.

He points his sword at BRAIDFUTE's *thrapple.*

Your life is forfeit.
It can be prolonged at will.   Tell!

BRAIDFUTE

I canna tell ye what I dinna ken.

HESELRIG

We'll see tomorrow what the pilliwinks
Can do.   Or the boot.   You like the boot,
Sir Thomas?   You are under arrest.
Take him away.

MIRREN

Uncle Tam!

BRAIDFUTE [*going*]

Hae nae fear, lass!   Wallace'll
Sune be back and sort this mackerel . . .

He is hurried out.

HESELRIG

Away!   Now, madam, you too
Can be arrested, on the same charge
Of sheltering an outlaw and a traitor.
The penalty, as you know, is death.
And, by law, you have already earned it—

MIRREN

He may be an outlaw;
Wallace is nae traitor.

HESELRIG

Enough of this bandying.
Tell me where he hides!

33

MIRREN

I canna! I winna!

HESELRIG

Oh, the madness! You know the consequences.
There is no one to help you. You are
Entirely dependent on my mercy—
And I would be merciful—but I have
My duty. You can help us both.
Tell me, woman! Or you will come with me!

MIRREN

I winna! Oh, Wallace, help me!

JEAN

Oh, my leddie!

At this, DONALD *bursts from the grip of the* TROOPERS *guarding him, and comes at* HESELRIG, *who runs him through with his sword.*

DONALD [*falls*]

Ah!

JEAN

Donald!

MIRREN *draws a dagger from her bosom.*

JEAN [*kneeling by* DONALD]

Donald!

DONALD *wreathes about, swoons.*

HESELRIG

Arrest her!

Two TROOPERS *grip* MIRREN. *She stabs one but is held by the other. She struggles.* HESELRIG'*s sword is pointed at her bosom.*

A wildcat from the heather, eh?   Do not
Struggle so, my dear; you may spoil
That pretty bosom for your outlaw.
He is not worth all this, I assure you.

MIRREN

Murderer!   Ye'll never find him
And he'll kill you as ye've killt Donald.

JEAN

No; he lives, my leddie.   Oh, Donald!   Here—

She gives him wine, tends him.

HESELRIG

Who cares about one churl more or less?
Impertinent dog! . . . You refuse to tell?
Your last chance, spitfire.
I can have you executed now
With perfect right.   I offer you
Your life for a word.

MIRREN

Never!   Never!   Never!

*With a supreme effort she breaks from her guard's grip and pitches
forward onto HESELRIG's swordpoint.   She gasps and falls.*

JEAN [*shrieks*]

Oh, my leddie!   Oh!   Oh!

HESELRIG [*to* MIRREN]

You mad creature!

Kneels by MIRREN

Why did you do that?

JEAN

You did it, ye murderin—Oh, my leddie!

HESELRIG

Stop that noise, girl, and fetch
Something to stanch her wound.
A cloth of some sort.

JEAN

Ay, sir.

Exit JEAN.

HESELRIG [*with wine*]

Now, my dear, some of this.

MIRREN *groans.* *Enter* JEAN *with clout.* *She unlatches* MIRREN'S
bodice, and stanches wound.

HESELRIG

Her eyes open.   Can you speak, madam?

JEAN *sobs.*

Be still, you fool girl, or leave the room.
Can you speak, Lady Mirren?
Where does Wallace hide?   Can you
Hear me?   Where does Wallace hide?
Try to speak now.   Tell me.   I am
Your friend.   Where does Wallace hide?

JEAN

Dinna speak, my leddie!   Oh, my leddie!

HESELRIG [*striking* JEAN]

Get out, or shut your mouth!
Lift her head.   Now.

He gives MIRREN *wine.*

MIRREN [*faintly*]

Wallace!

MIRREN *dies*.   JEAN *sobs wildly*.

HESELRIG [*standing*]

She is gone.   Madness, madness.
But it was an execution.
It is all a touch and go.
—Reform patrol in the street!

TROOPERS *move to lift* MIRREN.

JEAN

Oh, sir, no!   No!

HESELRIG

Stop that noise, I say; or you'll come with us.
Leave the body.   We must hurry
To the Castle—they may return
In strength and we cannot be burdened.
We have the old man.   Quick,
There is no time—by the back road.
And no noise!   Carry on!

Exeunt TROOPERS.

My compliments to Messire William.
Tell him this was an act of justice,
Despite my inclinations—
And to bring any complaints
To Lanark Castle tomorrow.
I will attend to them personally
And with pleasure.

Going, he stops, looking down at MIRREN.   *Then, quietly, to himself:*

Folly, folly.
Heselrig, this is war.

Exit HESELRIG.

[*From here, play slowly till* WALLACE's *entry*.]

JEAN [*kneeling by* MIRREN]

Oh, my leddie, my bonnie leddie!

JEAN *buries her face in her hands and turns her head away from the
corpse.*

DONALD

Jeanie!

JEAN *takes wine to* DONALD.

JEAN

Oh, Donald, I canna look on her.
I canna look on her, my bonnie leddie,
In her bluid liggin there.   Hae mair
O' this, lad.   Oh, Donald, Donald!

DONALD

Help me up, Jeanie!

He raises himself but falls back.

I canna.

JEAN [*tending him*]

Ligg ye quaet, Donald.   They're aa
Awa, nou.   Ye can dae nocht, nou.
Oh, my leddie, my bonnie leddie deid!
My bonnie wee leddie deid!
Oh, Donald, Donald!   Why has this to be?
Can they no lea us our lane?
Whar are the men?   Oh, Wallace,
Come back!

She goes to MIRREN.

Come back to my leddie!
My bonnie leddie deid! [*In paroxysm*] Oh! Oh!

Pause, JEAN *greiting.*

38

DONALD

I hear them, Jeanie.

JEAN [*running to entry, crying out*]

Wallace! Wallace! Wallace!

Enter WALLACE, GRAHAM, MURRAY, *with drawn swords.*

WALLACE

What's aa the steer? [*Seeing* MIRREN] Christ in heaven!

He kneels by her.

Mirren! Mirren!

GRAHAM

Leddie Mirren!

MURRAY

Wha did this, Jean?

JEAN

Oh, sir, sir!

GRAHAM

Does she live, Wallace?

WALLACE *looks up silently, his face answering* GRAHAM.

JEAN

Oh! Oh! Oh!

WALLACE [*slowly, quietly*]

Jean, what happen't? Whar's Sir Tam?

JEAN [*hysterical*]

They killt her! Oh sir, they killt her!
And they've taen Sir Tammas wi them, sir.
And Donald is skaithit sair, see!

39

WALLACE

Nou then, Jeanie, grip yoursel.
Puir Donald; brave lad! Tell me
What happen't, Jean. Christ, what hae I dune?
Oh, Mirren, Mirren!

He breaks down.

She begged me to byde! She's deid, Jean!
She begged me to byde! What happen't?

JEAN

Oh, sir, they cam ben and spierit at us,
Sir Tammas and my leddie. And they killt her.
She wadna tell. She wadna tell,
And they killt her—

MURRAY

Wha was it, Jean?
Were they robbers? Can ye mynd
Hou they lookit?

GRAHAM

Deils! Deils!

JEAN

It was the Shirra, sir!

WALLACE [*starting up*]

The Shirra? Heselrig? No!
Are ye shair, lassie? Donald, is she richt?

DONALD

Ay, it was himsel, wi the patrol.
He wad tak my leddie as hostage
To lure ye til the Castle . . .

She wadna gang, and in the strauch'e
Fell on Heselrig's sword—Oh, sir,
It was a noble leddie, rest her soul—

JEAN [*greiting wildly*]

He said to tell ye it was execution,
Sir, and justice for harbouring ye—
Though he didna want it, he said . . . .

WALLACE

The fiends frae hell! Wemen-fleshers!
And this the folk Tammas wad hae us
Treat wi! See to Donald, Jean—guid lassie.
Get him til his bed! I'll be in syne.

GRAHAM *goes to* DONALD *and examines his skaith.*

GRAHAM

Ach, it's no sae guid. And no sae bad,
Either. Ye'll live to revenge your leddie,
Donald. Come, Jean, we'll tak him ben.

Exeunt JEAN *and* GRAHAM, *supporting* DONALD.

WALLACE

Oh, Murray! See what liggs here!
Ah, Mirren, Mirren!

MURRAY

This will be
A barb in our side, Wallace. Nae peace
Wi this! War on wemen!

WALLACE

Mirren, Mirren!
Ah, Sir Tam, what think ye nou?
Guid Christ abune, Jesu, I sweir by the Rood
There shall nae peace be in this land

41

Till vengeance is dune. And nae rest, neither!
Murray, hie ye til Cairtlin Craigs—

MURRAY

Ay, man! Guid! Guid! Ah, Wallace—!

WALLACE

Bring doun twa score men, the best we hae.
Or the cock craw we visit Heselrig abed,
And mak siccar—and syne drive
The haill garrison frae Lanark, openlie.
The morn's morn, in the name o' John Balliol
King o' Scots, we declare open war
On Edward!

MURRAY

      Man, at last! Wallace,
My hairt lowps to hear this speak!

WALLACE

Lords or nae lords, this is war.
Nae quarter shall we gie, nae pitie shaw—
For her sake there shall ten thousand dee,
And I, Murray, insatiate o' bluid
Till this skaith is healed that's opened
In me nou, gowpin wide—ah, Mirren!—
Bluid will hae bluid, indeed, or vengeance'
Drouth is slockenit in Wallace—

MURRAY

Wallace, put the harness on your rage
And bend it for our purpose—This is a sign
Frae God, auld friend, to mettle us—

WALLACE

Guid Murray, ay, maybe ye're richt.
I'd liefer hae nae sign and her alive,

But God has willed it sae, it seems,
That a frail lassie's daith should gie barb
And spur til bluidie vengeance, war
Sleepless and pitiless.   We'll greit
Nae mair, but cry up daith and fire,
Destruction!   Ah, Mirren!   Here was
The maist beauteous flouer o' the flock,
Here was my luve, here Scotland
Incarnate, the White Rose breathin
In a lassie's form, cauld nou and spreitless,
But a queen, laurelled wi her daith
And wi her ain reid bluid anointit—
A fell sacrifice to bless a war.
No, she isna deid, but lives in me,
To airm my bluidie hand, and skail
Aa mercie frae the hairt wi the great
Storm o' her sillic daith.   I am
Become a priest, Murray, a dedicate
Wi ae crusade—deliverance!

He picks up the clout stained with MIRREN'S *bluid.*

This, sweet-hairt, will be our gonfalon
And standart, aye in the van o' battle,
First to view wir victories and last
To leave defeat.   Vengeance is mine,
Saith the Lord—and sae says Wallace wicht!
Nou, haste ye, Murray, til the Craigs.
We hae work the morn.

MURRAY

                    I'se get the Graham.
Guid Wallace, sleep.   We'se need aa wir strenth.
And yours.   Till first licht then.

Exit MURRAY.

43

WALLACE [*kneeling, gazing at her*]

Ah, Mirren, Mirren, Mirren!

WALLACE *lifts* MIRREN *in his arms and exit slowly, as lights dim slowly out.   The stage is empty.*

Here may follow an INTERVAL, during which the CHRON-ICLERS *or their* SERVITORS *can clear away the candelabra, tassies, basket of washing, etc., and rearrange table, kist, stools, etc., for Act II.   If no Interval is preferred, this action should be transferred to the beginning of Act II.*

ACT II

Enter the CHRONICLERS, *with* DONALD, *and such* SERVITORS *as may be needful, carrying five shields blazoned with the arms of Scotland, Balliol, Wallace, MacDuff, and Graham; a Scottish Royal Standard;* WALLACE'*s own personal standard (gules, a lyon rampant, argent); a spear with* MIRREN'*s Bluidie Clout attached to it as a guidon; a rolled-up Saltire flag; some pewter drinking-vessels; and any other articles that may be required. Assisted by* DONALD *and* SERVITORS, *the* CHRONICLERS *hang the shields up in a row on the back wall. They speak their lines while setting the scene, and when they have done, the* SCOTS CHRONICLER *shakes out the Saltire, and, with a flourish, spreads it over the table.*

SCOTS CHRONICLER

And sae William the Wallace did slay the English Sheriff of Lanark and syne hystit the standart of the Lyon. [*Here he sets up the Scottish Royal Standard.*] Frae this time there gaithert til his force all thae that were in bitter spreit and owrehailit with the yoke of English thirldom, and Wallace dung doun the Sudron allwhare and his micht and pouer increasit dailie. Syne he cuist himsel to tak the castles and strang haulds whar the Sudron was lord, that he micht free the Kingrik frae her enemies.

The rebellious Scots were now mightily enlarged and proceeded about the country not secretly as before but openly, committing murders, arsons, pillage, and other injuries against the King's Peace, putting to the sword all English that they could find and turning themselves afterwards to the siege of the castles. So King Edward sent forth a great army that the rebels might be confounded and the King's Peace restored.

It was on the tenth day of September in the year of grace ae thousand, twa hunder and ninetie-sevin that Wallace and his host passit til Stirling at the Brig of Forth and there met with the English in dour battle, and the Scots bare aff the victorie. The maist pairt of the Sudron airmie was slain, some pitten til the sword and ithers drounit in the waters of Forth. This did William the Wallace at Stirling Brig and of this had great renoun, sae that by consent of the haill folk he was made Guairdian of the Realm in the name of John of Balliol, King of Scots. All-throu the Kingrik he passt and put all Englishmen furth of Scotland. Syne intil England with his host and bade there til Yule.

In that time the praise of God ceased in all the monasteries and churches of the whole province from Newcastle-upon-Tyne to Carlisle. For all the monks, the canons regular, and the other priests, the servants of the Lord, with almost the whole people, had fled before the face of the Scots. Thus they had liberty for fire and rapine from Saint Luke's Day until Martinmas. Then did King Edward in his wrath gather the greatest army that ever had been seen and in the spring of the next year did march north himself to extirpate the perfidious Scots. But the brigand William Wallace did constantly retreat before him, cravenly refusing to do battle, burning and laying waste the country as he went, so that the English should find no provender nor no place of refuge in Scotland.

SCOTS CHRONICLER

Abune the toun of Fawkirk, the Wallace [*here* DONALD *sets up the Bluidie Clout*] had set his camp in the Tor Wuid, and here he lay, this Eve of Sanct Mary Magdalene, byding his time till Edward's strength, by hunger and sickness, should be wastit all away. . . .

Exeunt CHRONICLERS *and* SERVITORS.

Sounds of troops carousing, off, distant trumpets, etc. Enter, all in helmets, WALLACE, MACDUFF, *and* GRAHAM, *followed by* ARMOUR-BEARERS *carrying two-handed swords, etc. First taking off their helmets, and handing them to* DONALD, WALLACE *and* MAC- DUFF *sit colloguing, with scrolled map, at table;* GRAHAM *paces restlessly up and down.* DONALD *serves bread and wine (maybe from kist, at back), then sits down on the ground, or on a stool, and cleans armour, or feathers arrows from a goose's wing. Evening.*

MACDUFF [*breaking bread*]

Set doun, Graham, can ye no? Wha can
Think wi you up and doun, up and doun,
Like a pent beast aa the day?

GRAHAM

Juist what I feel like, MacDuff.
A pent beast—aa the time.
Hou lang is this to last, Wallace,
Hou lang?

WALLACE

            Ye ken fine. Tak aff your gless,
John, and be wyce. Ah, I miss my Murray
That put reins on ye. My guid brave Murray;
An auld heid on young shouthers—

47

Murray wad gree wi me at the waste o't!
Retreat, retreat, retreat, nae action
But burnin aathing in our wake—
Reik, reik, reik—aye the fire at our back.
It was fine burnin the touns ayont Tweed
But no wir ain. Och, I ken why for,
But I dinna like it. Retreat, retreat—
Can I no hae twa dozen men, Wallace,
Nae mair, for a bit scrimmaging,
Even the baggage train?

WALLACE

Edward has nae baggage train—gin he has,
There's pickle ye'll find it cairryin.
Set doun, John. We're weirin him doun;
He's at his limit. Sune he'll turn
And gang back the wastit road he's come,
His tail atweesh his hurdies like a skelpit tyke,
Then, my lad, we faa upon him like a tempest
And destroy him utterlie, for ever.

GRAHAM

Ay, it's fine. I ken. But when, Wallace, when?

WALLACE

We can wale our ain time; we ken
His muvements, but he doesna ken ours.
To meet him in open field is suicide,
As weill ye ken.—Gin we had horse,
Ah then, my goshawk, hear a different tale!
—But we haena, bar the Comyn's maybe a hunder
Agane Edward's thousands. And weill ye ken yon,
Tae; sae set ye doun and tak your gless
Like a wyce laddie.

MACDUFF

                Ay, come on, John,
Ye'll hae action sune eneuch.
Edward canna last a week.
And syne—ah, Wallace, syne!

WALLACE

Ay, wi Edward broke in battle,
Ah, MacDuff, we can lift our heids again.

MACDUFF

We'll need the King, then.   D'ye hear ocht
Of Balliol?

WALLACE

                Ay, in France, by Edward's order,
Edward's prisoner.

GRAHAM

                He'll never return.
We ken.   We talk, but we aa ken
Balliol's dune.   Wallace, gin ye dinna
Tak the Croun, there's be domestic war
In Scotland.   Bruce nor Comyn can see
The tither on the throne and live,
Or let live.   Tak ye the Croun and haud it
Wi the sword.   The folk are wi ye.

WALLACE

Graham, I loe ye like a brither.
As a warrior I wad put ye mang
The first o' Christendie.
But as a statesman ye're a bab
At the breist, a bonnie bab

To feed wi bonnie comfits
And syne sleep sound.

MACDUFF

He's wyce tae, Wallace.   The bab kens
What's guid for'm—and the best for Scotland
Nou wad be Wallace King of Scots—

Noises off.   Enter ROBERT BRUCE, EARL OF CARRICK, *in armour.*

WALLACE

Carrick, this is guid!   Come ben, my lord.

BRUCE

Should I say " Your Majestie "?

WALLACE [*laughing*]

A stoup o' wine?

BRUCE

D'ye aim at the Croun, Wallace?

WALLACE

Hae dune wi the blethers, Bruce.   I'm blyth
Ye've come.   We need ye wi us—

BRUCE

I juist heard MacDuff, uncle to great Fife himsel
That crouns aa Kings o' Scots, say " Wallace "—

WALLACE

A jest, my lord.   MacDuff's joco.
We hae mair wechtie maitters for ye—

BRUCE

There's been rumours o' this afore,
But ne'er afore hae I—Wallace,
Speak me soothfastlie.   D'ye aim at the Croun?

WALLACE

By the Rood, ye think it, Bruce, I see!
Hear, then! I fecht for Scotland
And her richtfu King—wha-e'er he be.
Balliol is crounit King o' Scots.   No Bruce.
Gin Bruce had wan the judgment—

BRUCE

My guidsir didna win.   Balliol wan.
Balliol is King o' Scots, but Balliol's
A tuim tabard, as they say.   Balliol's dune.
Wallace is Guairdian o' Scotland
In Balliol's name, but Wallace rules.

WALLACE

My lord, there maun be governance.
Wha's to govern gin it isna me?
Edward? Comyn? Bruce? Wha?
Are we, this ancient folk and proud,
To thole the Sudron yoke and creep
And hide like huntit beasts acause
Our richtfu king's an exiled dowfart
And his rival Bruce, anither Achilles
In the field, skouks like Achilles
In his tent for jalousie?   I am nae king
Nor wish to be.   But tell me this—
Was Bruce's sword at Stirling Brig?
Was Comyn's?   Balliol's?

BRUCE

                    Bruce's couldna be.

51

WALLACE

Wha cuist the Sudron owre the Tweed
And herried his norrart lands last winter?
Wha sits here in the Torwuid under airms
And bydes till the fruit is ripe
To gaither the bluidie hairvest in—?

BRUCE

Ay, and wha scrieves his letters bauld
In the name of the Scots Estaits and gies,
Like a king, protection wi his writ?
Wha cries the barons til a pairliament?
Wha levies taxes, punishes and frees
At will? The King? Does Balliol scrieve?
Or William Wallace in his pride, but with nae
Tittle o' authoritie or " Yea " or " Nay "
Frae the anointit King his sel?

WALLACE

                                    Wha then's to dae't?
You, Lord Carrick? Bruce, I tell ye soothlie,
Gin ye wish the pouer ye can hae't!
Bring the Carrick chivalrie in! Command
The airmie o' Scotland in the field!
I'll serve under ye blyth eneuch.
And all here. Wad ye no?

MACDUFF

Blythlie, Carrick. Me and mine.
Graham, tae, I ken—

GRAHAM

                    My sword is Wallace's.
Gin Wallace mairch wi Bruce, there find me—

But, O my lords, this brand is roustin fast,
Wants Sudron bluid to slocken it.   Gie us
Action, by'r Leddie, or my heid is gray,
I beg ye—see my lyart locks!

WALLACE

Ha! Donald, wine for Sir John to cool him,
Him and his lyon looks—!

DONALD

Ay, Sir Weelum.   But I dout
It winna dowse the Graham's fire—

GRAHAM

Fire! Fire! Ye're richt, Donald.   Here's to fire!

WALLACE [*to* DONALD]

Ay, and for Lord Carrick, tae,
To fire his doutin hairt.

DONALD
My lord?

BRUCE

Ay, ay, some wine.   Be thankit.

WALLACE

But there's our answer, Bruce. Tak the command,
Drive out Edward til his ain domain
And sit in Scone as King o' Scots—and auld
MacDuff is here to hae ye crounit richtfullie. . . .
Dae this, my lord, and ilka chiel
In the Torwuid here will hail ye,
Follow ye, and dee for ye.

Ay, I see. . . .

Pause. DONALD *lights candles.*

WALLACE

Weill . . . ?

Pause.

BRUCE

The time isna ripe.

WALLACE

It's ripe for Edward, ripe for Wallace—
Wad it were ripe for you and aa the lords!
But no! They'd liefer fecht wi Edward
Agane me, nor wi me agane Edward—
As they've dune or this, and as you've dune
Yoursel, Bruce. There's feck o' guid Scots bluid
Ye've let for the bonnie een o' Edward—
Or they fecht the tane wi tither like tykes,
Like you and Comyn fecht, bleedin
The land til beggarie for pride
—And ye speak til me o' pride!

BRUCE

Wallace, ye speak like a bairn!
Ye dinna ken the hauf o't.
I, like ither lords, hae peace wi Edward;
We hae lands and folk in England tae,
And for them we awe him fealtie
And homage as liege knichts, and richtfullie.
Wad ye hae us break our solemn
Knichtlie vows, [*snapping his fingers*] like that?

WALLACE

Ho, ho! We haud til our solemn vows nou!
We respect a sworn aith as weill!

54

And when last did a Scottish or an English
Or a French or ither Norman lord
Haud til his bunden word gin it didna
Suit him, juist?

GRAHAM

Has King Edward, even?

MACDUFF

Has Bruce til Balliol?

WALLACE

Ach, I giena
A horse's turd for a baron's aith
Till Edward of England sall keep his
An hour efter it irks him.

BRUCE

Aiths may be broken under duress,
But no wi impunitie—

WALLACE

Is invasion of Scotland duress, Bruce?
Or is it impunitie?

BRUCE

Edward has our hostages.
No a lord that put his seal on the Roll
But gied a hostage for guid conduct.
My ain faither is in England.   Am I
To raise banners agane my ain house?

WALLACE

Is Scotland no worth the life o' an auld man?

MACDUFF

My hostage, Carrick, is a bairn, my son;
I am here in airms agane his jailer.
Ye can stand wi me, my lord, can ye no?
And at wee-er cost—an auld man and a bairn!

WALLACE

Monie a man has deed, my lord,
And monie mair will dee or Scotland
Breathes free air again.   Ay, and monie
A woman, tae. . . .   See yon standart!
Yon's a lassie's bluid that blazons it.

BRUCE

I ken.   Ay, Wallace, I hae heard o' yon.
It was a fell deed.

WALLACE

                    Is this the liege lord
Ye serve? I'm tellt your Sudron cronies,
Even, taunt ye wi fylin your hands
In the bluid o' your countrymen.   It's truth!

BRUCE *looks at his hands in silence.*

I shouldna said it. Forgie me. It is unsaid.
But, my lord, bethink ye o' the richt
And truth o' this.   Come owre wi us
And help us skail this pestilence frae the land!

GRAHAM

Why for can Edward no be content wi's ain?
Isna England wide and fair eneuch
But he maun come here and herrie us
That never did him ill or thocht on't?

Bruce, ye maun ken we canna treat wi'm.
Edward has nae honour but his greed.
We wish nae pickle of English grund;
We fecht but for wir ain, and for the semple
Richt o' a folk to mynd wir ain affeirs
As we will—athout the help o' neibours.
Let Edward gang back and mynd his.   We'd
Suner our bannocks brunt than he should turn them.

BRUCE [*after a pause*]

Ay.

WALLACE

My lord, is Scotland less nor Annandale
And Carrick?   Is honour less nor interest?
Bruce, answer me this, and we hae nae
Mair to say.

BRUCE

Wallace, I canna
Be wi ye, while Balliol is King
And the Reid Comyn in your camp.
We can nae mair mak comitie
Nor tyke wi swine.   Our enmitie
Is ower auld and ower deep for truce.

WALLACE

It canna sleep for Scotland's sake?

BRUCE

For honour's sake.

WALLACE

—A commoditie!
Like land or title, wi its price.
Ye taunt me wi wish to be King.
You could be King!

57

Or Comyn.

WALLACE

Suner either nor Edward.

BRUCE

This is whar we break, Wallace.
We wad suner Edward nor the tither.

WALLACE

Whiles I despair. Whiles I wonder
Wha made the word "nobilitie" but a noble,
As a lunátic cries he's the King.

BRUCE

We canna serve under ye, Wallace,
Nae mair nor could ye under a tapster.
Ye hae nae rank.

WALLACE

                    Rank, rank, rank! Yon's the word!
Ay, rank is rank indeed, my lord! I hae
Its stink in my neb. Gie me tapsters!
Donald, be you tapster, and some wine.

BRUCE [*rising, hand on sword*]

Wallace!

WALLACE

Ay, I mean it. I mean black shame
On ye, Carrick, and on your kith
And kin and ilka renegade lord in the land
Whase rank can kneel til the fause Plantagenet
And devour his ain flesh and bluid
For rank's sake. Ay, rank indeed!

BRUCE

Wallace, ye try me owre far—

BRUCE *draws sword*.

MACDUFF

Carrick!

GRAHAM [*drawing*]

My lord, I pray ye—

BRUCE

A Bruce will tak nae sic words frae onie man—

WALLACE

I fear ye nocht, my lord.   I hae rank
Tae, as Guairdian o' Scotland,
And I am mang my ain folk that gied it me.
Ye're alien here, my lord, though fain
It werena sae.   Put up your sword.

BRUCE *subsides*.

I hae nae fecht wi you.   I fecht
Wi Sudrons.   Bruce, there is a battle nigh,
A week or less, when Edward turns for hame.
With you, we could win.   Wantin ye
We could loss.   Here, nou!   Will ye
Gie me a true word and band?

BRUCE

Speak and I'll tell ye.

WALLACE

Gin ye winna come in wi us
Will ye come nocht agane us?
The Carrick chivalrie could swing
The tide ae road or tither.   I need to ken.

59

I'll say this.   Ye've sawn a seed of doubt.
Maybe ye're richt.   I'll think on thir things.
I hae a peace wi Edward.   Byde till
Its term come Candlemas.   Byde in the field
Till my airm is free, Wallace, and we'll
Speak again.   Maybe wi ither outcome.
I hae monie lealties.   I gang
For Ayr, nou.   I sall keep the castle there
For Edward, as is my dutie—and frae Edward,
As is the tither dutie.   Guid nicht, sirs.

WALLACE

I haena lang to byde, Bruce.   Maybe
'Tis owre late e'en nou.   Or owre sune.
But gin ye keep Edward out of Ayr
'Twill be smaa aid til him.

BRUCE

We'll see.   Guid nicht.

WALLACE

Guid nicht, my lord.   Donald,
Guaird for Lord Carrick!

DONALD

Ay, Sir Weelum.

Exit DONALD.   *Trumpet, off.*

MACDUFF

Guid nicht, my lord.

GRAHAM

My lord.

Exit BRUCE.

The Bruce is gey like the chiel
Our Saviour tellt to sell aa he had
And gie til the puir folk.

MACDUFF

Bruce? Hou d'ye mean?

GRAHAM

He gaed waefullie awa,
For he had muckle possessions.

MACDUFF

He's a loss for aa that. Pray God
Comyn doesna think the like.

GRAHAM

Weill he micht. He hasna liftit
A finger yet.

WALLACE

           In the end, my friends,
We've nane but the folk; they've nocht
To loss but life and libertie.
But gin we've them, we've aa. They're Scotland,
Nane ither. The pouer of e'en the greatest lord,
Like Bruce, is nocht in the end but the folk
He leads. They micht be beat in battle,
Slain in thousands, conquered and thirlit—
But no for aye. Spring maun follow winter.
The Romans cam and gaed. Sae will Edward.
Ah, Alexander, come again!

Enter DONALD, *in haste.*

GRAHAM [*laughing*]

Alexander was cried on, and Donald chosen!

61

DONALD

And Alexander has come, Sir John.
Sandie Fraser, Sir Weelum—

MACDUFF

Ah, Sandie the scout.   Bring him in, Donald,
What're ye bydin for?

DONALD

He's gey fordune,
My lord; he's gettin a bit piece
And a dram.

WALLACE

He'll get his piece
And his cup here. Donald, bring him in
And haud your clash.

DONALD

Ay, Sir Weelum.

Exit DONALD.

WALLACE

The discipline in this camp
Is kin o' carefree, sirs.

GRAHAM

What can ye expect, wi this idleset?
The men are restless, Wallace.
They've nocht to fill their time wi,
I wish ye'd let me—

WALLACE

Graham, hae I no tellt ye—?

Enter DONALD *with* SANDIE FRASER.

Here, sir.

Come ben, lad.

Sandie Fraser the scout, sir, ye mynd—

Ay, I mynd weill, Sandie.   Set ye doun.
Donald, gie'm his cogie. . . . Nou, Sandie,
Tell us, what did ye see?   First,
What length's the Sudron wan til?

Sir, yesternicht he lay at Kirkliston
And the day he passed through Linlithgie—

Never! Linlithgow! No a dozen mile aff!

Ay, and he comes on.   And siccan
A host ye never saw.   They say
Three thousand horse.   And hauf a score
O' men-at-airms for ilka mountit knicht.
And the Welsh has new bows a man's lenth
Wi arrows a yaird lang. . . .   But they're
Fell and dowie for aa that.

                Nae wonner.
Ye couldna feed a quarter o' yon
On the kintra the wey it is nou—

WALLACE

Tell us mair, lad.

SANDIE

He kens ye're here.

GRAHAM

He canna tell! Hou can he ken?

SANDIE

He's gey short o' vivers
And was for turnin for Embro.
Then yestreen twa knichts rade in
And tauld ye were in the Torwuid.

GRAHAM

Traitorie! Wha was it, Sandie?

MACDUFF

No the first time, John. And no the last.

WALLACE

Gaun on, Sandie.

SANDIE

When he heard,
The King was gey joco, and praisit God
That had deliverit ye intil his hands
In the nick o' time. He took back
The order o' retreat he'd pitten out,
And said he'd come up wi ye and fecht
Ye the morn's morn. The news was pit about
Wi trumpets through the camp to cheer them.
They were fell laich at hairt,
I'm tellin ye, and no muckle better
For the news—for ye canna cat news—

64

D'ye ken wha were the knichts betrayit us, Sandie?

SANDIE

No, Sir Weelum. Some say it was Blackbaird
Was ane o'm—

GRAHAM

   Blackbaird? The Earl Patrick!
He was aye Edward's man. Traitor Scots!
They'se get their fairin!

WALLACE

    They will that, John . . .
Linlithgow. Three league aff. Graham,
MacDuff, my lads, the fruit is ripe
Upon the tree. And I jalouse 'twill faa
The morn's morn, and we'll be there
To gaither it in. Och, gin I had horse!
Nou, Sandie lad, tell us aa ye can.

SANDIE

They're desperate for want o' victual, Sir Weelum.
Yestreen, efter the news cam in, the King
Gied them wine to pit hairt in them,
But it didna work out richt, for they got
Fechtin wi ither owre the casks,
Welsh agane English and monie deid,
And the Welsh are sayin they winna fecht
The Scots wi tuim kytes, and there's nocht
But wine to full them wi. The King
Onwaits ships in the Forth wi food and gear
But they've never cam. He was for gangin
Back, but nou he'll fecht. I ran the haill
Road, Sir Weelum, to tell ye. My faither
Said for ye to mynd o' him when ye're King.

WALLACE [*laughing*]

Ay, Sandie, I'll mynd weill, and ye'll
Byde here wi me and bluid your spear
For Scotland's King.   Nou get some sleep;
Ye've dune weill, lad.   See tae'm, Donald.

DONALD

Ay, sir.   Come awa, Sandie.

GRAHAM

And, Donald!   Tell the guairds frae me
To skail aa wemen and followers
Frae the camp.   Get them awa
Intil the wuid.   We fecht the morn.

DONALD

Ay, Sir John.

Exeunt DONALD *and* SANDIE.

WALLACE

MacDuff, will ye spier at
The Reid Comyn and the Stewart
To step by?   We maun hae counsel on this.

MACDUFF

I'll dae that.

Exit MACDUFF.   *Trumpet.*

GRAHAM

Man, this is news!   At last!
Nou we can meet them.   " Baird til baird "
Was your cry at Stirling, Wallace;
It sall be again, and victorie again,
And this time a king fleein afore our banners!

He brandishes the Bluidie Clout.

And vengeance doublie sweet.   Aha!

Enter MACDUFF.

MACDUFF

John, ye're a wild tink.

WALLACE

I tellt ye the time was ripe, John,
Did I no?

GRAHAM

Ay, ripe!

MACDUFF

Comyn and Stewart
Were on their road here, Wallace.   They've heard
The news.   And they've Stewart's uncle,
Menteith, wi'm.

WALLACE

We sall see.

Enter a GUARD.

GUARD

Sir John Comyn, sir, and the Stewart—

Enter SIR JOHN COMYN, SIR JOHN STEWART OF BONKILL, *and* SIR
JOHN MENTEITH.

WALLACE

Come ben, sirs.   It's guid to hae ye
Wi's, Menteith.   Ye'll hae heard
That Edward lies at Linlithgow?

COMYN

Ay, we cam as sune's we heard.
Wallace, we maun confer.

Enter DONALD.

WALLACE

                    Deed, ay.
We fecht the morn's morn.   Some wine, sirs.
Set ye doun.   Edward has three thousand horse.
I jalouse a like number o' Welsh bowmen
Wi the new lang bow I dinna like the sound o'.
Hou monie horse hae ye, Comyn?

COMYN

Ae hunder and twa-score.

MENTEITH [*to* DONALD]

Na, na; nae wine for me.
I've anither hunder, Wallace,
On condition—

STEWART

                    Uncle, leave this, will ye?

WALLACE

What's this, sirs?

COMYN

                    Wallace,
This brooks nae delay.   Wha's to command?

WALLACE

I dinna tak your drift, Comyn?
Ilkane his ain chivalrie, o' course.

COMYN

I mean in chief—

GRAHAM

Wha ither but Wallace?

Graham, be still.   What exactlie
D'ye mean, Comyn?

MENTEITH

He means
It's no seemlie for barons o' rank
To serve under your command, Wallace,
A landless man.   Stewart has precedence.

GRAHAM [*drawing sword*]

Menteith!

MACDUFF [*knocking down* GRAHAM'S *sword*]

Put up your sword, Graham!
This is nae bairns' ploy.

MENTEITH

Ye're richt, MacDuff.
I say the Stewart should hae command.
You are grown owre big wi war, Wallace.
Nou is the time for wycer heids
To mak the peace aa Scotland's bleedin for.
Stewart is wi me for peace, and Stewart
Has precedence.   Ye maun gie owre the command!

WALLACE

Peace?   Wi Edward chappin at the door?
This is midsimmer blethers.   Menteith, what ails ye?
There can be nae peace but efter victorie,
And nae victorie wiout battle,
And the battle is the morn's morn—
This is a council o' war, is it no?
Let us speak o' battle.   We want horse.

MENTEITH

Ye've heard my terms, Wallace.
On nane ither, ye hae my chivalrie.

STEWART

I've nae pairt wi this, Wallace.
Ye hae my sword and my foresters
Wiout condition, freelie—

COMYN

I'm wi Menteith.   My terms are his.

WALLACE

Sirs, we canna win wi nae horse.
Whar then's your peace, Menteith?
Our schiltroms o' spearmen can maybe
Break the Sudron chivalrie, but wantin
Reserve o' horse his bowmen can
And will destroy us.   We'll canna
Win near them.   They'll dominate the field.

STEWART

Comyn, uncle, this puts me
In a stead I deem unworthie.
I'm nae bairn to hae words said for me.
Wallace, I hae nae wish for command.
Sirs, Wallace has sauvit Scotland aince,
At Stirling Brig, and dealt her enemies
A stound they winna forget in a while,
And he'll can sauf her again, and finallie.
He, wi thir guid knichts, has stude
Alane when aa was tint.   What thanks
Is this, when aa hings on this last cast,
To higgle like auld wifes at a stall
For precedence—?

I saw Bruce leavin the camp.   Why for
Was he here?   Is he wi ye?   Wallace,
Hae ye a band wi Bruce?

WALLACE

Bruce isna wi us, and I hope
He's no agane us.

GRAHAM

Bruce is neither
Het nor cauld, and all sic Laodiceans
I'd puke out my mouth—

COMYN

Hae ye a band wi Bruce?
Wad ye hae him crounit King at Scone,
MacDuff?

GRAHAM

Wad you be King, Comyn?

COMYN

I hae mair richt nor onie Bruce—

WALLACE

Graham, I bid ye be still.   Edward
Is our enemie.   Comyn, I hae
Nae band wi Bruce.   My king is Balliol.

COMYN

Balliol!

MACDUFF

Sirs, may I hae a word?   I hae lived
Langer nor you and maybe hae langer sicht.

Edward liggs at Linlithgow.   The morn
We fecht.   Maybe we dee.   Can we no
Offput this talk o' King o' Scots
Till the King o' England's furth o' Scotland
And his airmie broken on the field?

STEWART
MacDuff is richt.

MENTEITH
Is Stewart to command?

GRAHAM
Wallace—

WALLACE
Sirs, we are agreed, then, that we fecht
The morn?   There's can be nae retreat.
Guid.   Weill then, we sax are here
Commanders.   Let us draw up our plan
And divide the command.   Comyn, you
And Menteith has the chivalrie; Stewart
His foresters atween the spearmen
'Rayit in fowr schiltroms, their spears
Like hurchins, birslin point owre point,
The fangit scaurs wharon the sea
O' Edward's chivalrie will dash—
And break.   We haud back the horse till then.
Syne, you Comyn, and Menteith, frae ilka wing,
Breenge doun and crush the bowmen;
The schiltroms are lowsit on the stricken
Host and the day is ours.   Ilkane here
Will haud his ain command and the victorie
Be common.   Nor mine nor yours but Scotland's.
Are we gree'd?   And Scotland's peace
Will follow at its back, Menteith.

72

And Bruce?

WALLACE

Bruce winna be wi us.
He has his peace wi Edward.
He winna fecht.

STEWART

I gree.   Uncle—

MENTEITH [*after a pause*]

We'll see the morn.

GRAHAM

The morn will be owre late.

MENTEITH

We'll see the morn.   I say nae mair.

WALLACE

Comyn, ye'll be wi us?   Gif no,
Wantin your chivalrie, I'd fain draw aff
Intil the wuid and gar Edward
Gang back as he was tendin.
He's stairvin.   He canna last a week.

MACDUFF

He's owre near at hand
For drawin aff nou, Wallace.

WALLACE

Ay, I dout
Ye're richt.   We maun juist stand and hope
To haud him and maybe keep a force

In being and gang ayont Forth
And gaither strenth again.
Nocht ither rests wi's. Wi you, Comyn,
And Menteith, or even you wiout
Menteith, we could win, under God
And the richt.   Wantin ye, we canna.
We can juist stand and dee.

COMYN

A joint command?

WALLACE

   Ay.

GRAHAM

     Daft! Plain daft!

COMYN

Wallace, you are Guairdian o' Scotland.
My condition is this.   Nae truck wi Bruce.
I to be joint Guairdian wi Stewart,
A triumvirate wi support o' my richt
Til the Croun.   But gin we fail the morn—

GRAHAM

Fail—?

COMYN

     Gin we fail, then you, Wallace,
To dispone the Guairdianship—

WALLACE

Nane but the Scots Estaits
Can promise yon, Comyn.

COMYN

I'm seekin juist your support,
Wallace, or your decedence.

STEWART

This is no richt!

COMYN

It is my condition.

WALLACE

It seems
I can dae nocht but gree, Comyn.
For your twa hunder horse, yours and Menteith's,
I gree.   We'se pledge on that, then?
Stewart!   Menteith?

MENTEITH

And Stewart
Has command hereafter.

STEWART

I refuse.
Ye hae nae richt—

GRAHAM

There's your answer, Menteith.

MACDUFF

Sirs, sirs!   Let us hae nae mair debate
But byde the tide o' battle.

MENTEITH

Graham
Has a bauld gab.   Has he a sword
As lang's his tongue?

75

COMYN

Menteith!

GRAHAM [*drawing*]

Ye could try, Menteith!

WALLACE

Graham, put up your sword! I'll hae
Nae fechtin in my tent. Menteith,
Forgie him; it is late.

MENTEITH

This is no the end
O' the tale. Guid nicht. Come, Stewart.

Exit MENTEITH.

WALLACE

We convene at dawn, sirs.

STEWART

Guid nicht, Wallace.
It is Menteith ye maun forgie.
He reckons honour in mealie-bags.

Trumpet.

COMYN

At dawn, then.

WALLACE

At dawn. For Scotland.

Exeunt COMYN *and* STEWART.

MACDUFF

A bad business.

WALLACE

It could be waur.
We've tint Menteith, but Comyn's wi us.

GRAHAM

Maybe Comyn's wi us.

MACDUFF

I think no.

WALLACE

We'll see.

Pause.

GRAHAM

Our star is set—

MACDUFF

Graham, yon's an ill word!

WALLACE

Never! Graham, this is no like you.
Get some sleep, lad.

GRAHAM

Caitiffs, pultroons,
Reneggers! Ah, Scotland, what vipers
Thou suckles in thy bosom!

MACDUFF

Scotland is mair nor Comyn and Menteith.

WALLACE

Graham, lad, what we hae e'en nou
Is our victorie.   Gin we all dee the morn

And the battle lost, the war is aye wan.
The war was wan at Stirling Brig last year
And weill Edward kens it. We pruvit then
The micht of feudal England can be checked,
Owreset and humbelt by the folk o' Scotland
Wi nae lords, nae ither help, their lane.
Win or loss the morn canna
Cheynge yon—for what's dune aince
Can eith be dune again. Yon's our strenth
And yon's our bydin victorie. Nou
I maun sleep, and ye tae.

MACDUFF

Ay, true. God be wi ye, Will—

WALLACE

And wi Scotland, the morn's morn,

GRAHAM

By the Rood, she's need o' the Lord's help
All richt; she'll get nane frae her ain lords,
I dout.

WALLACE [*laughing*]
Awa til your beds. We'll need
Shairp een forbye shairp swords the morn.

Exeunt MACDUFF *and* GRAHAM. WALLACE *sits at table, thinking, head in hands. Exit* DONALD *with wine-cups and jugs. Lights dim.*

WALLACE

The morn . . .

Pause. Suddenly he starts up, staring, as if he sees a spectre. Here MIRREN, *her breast stained with blood, can walk silently through audience and across the stage, or* WALLACE *can merely imagine her, whichever the Director prefers.*

Mirren! Mirren! What omen is this?

No respond.

I shall nocht fail ye!

He seizes the Bluidie Clout and brandishes it.

Thow is avengit!

As in a dwaum, he stumbles after her across the stage. Exit MIRREN.

My tender babe.

Enter DONALD.

DONALD

Sir Weelum! Ye're like as ye're walkin
In a dwaum. What ails ye? By your wild looks
Ye micht hae seen a ghaist—

DONALD takes the Bluidie Clout from WALLACE.

WALLACE

Ay, maybe I did, Donald.

He puts his arm round DONALD's *shoulders, and together they move
slowly towards the exit.*

Maybe I did, tae. I'm wearie. Come on!

Exeunt WALLACE *and* DONALD. *The stage is empty.*

ACT III

Enter the two CHRONICLERS, *with such* SERVITORS *as may be needful. Whiles working, whiles speaking, they remove all shields, banners, etc., displayed in Act II.*

ENGLISH CHRONICLER

And so at Falkirk, on the Maudlyn Day, King Edward fought the Scots and made great slaughter of his enemies. The craven Scottish chivalry fled without so much as breaking a lance, yea, without joining battle, but many thousand foot were left dead upon the field. After his great victory the King might remain no longer in Scotland, for the ships that he awaited had not come and in no place was there store or plenty. Soon therefore he returned to England and made pilgrimages to holy tombs, thanking God for his victory, as was his custom after such business.

SCOTS CHRONICLER

A short while after this grievous battle at Fawkirk, because he had failit in his chairge, Sir William Wallace of his ain free will disponit the office of Guairdian of Scotland, and walit suner to serve with the folk, as he said, than be set in authoritie owre them for their ruin. Syne aince mair King Edward invadit the liberties of the Kingrik and this time brocht all the lords of

80

Scotland, baith great and lesser men, intil his peace, sauf but the Wallace that lay in the forest, and Sir William Oliphant, a young squire, that keepit the Castel of Stirling for the Lyon and wad nocht bend til the King. Sae Edward set himself fornent the walls and wad ding them doun with divers michtie ingines.

The King was much vexed at the obstinacy of this Citadel of Stirling and deployed against it all his great engines, the Gloucester, the Vicar, the Belfrey, the Parson, the Tout-le-Monde, and others, thirteen in number, and urgently commanded the despatch from London of the greatest of them all, the War Wolf, which he needed for the reduction of such a strength. At last, on the twenty-fourth day of July, the year of grace one thousand, three hundred and four, after three months' siege, the garrison capitulated and the King's relief and joy was manifest. [*Sounds of merriment, off.*] He commanded a great banquet in celebration of his final triumph, and made merry here with his ladies and the whole court assembled. . . .

Enter, through audience, a MAJOR DOMO, *followed by* PAGE-BOYS *and* COURT SERVANTS, *carrying rich hangings, two chairs of state, which they place on the deis at back, baskets of fruit, wine, clean drinking vessels, etc. Directed by the* MAJOR DOMO, *some of the* SERVANTS *clear away candle-sticks, maps, etc. The* SCOTS CHRONICLER *removes the Saltire flag from the table and reverently folds it up; more sounds of merriment are heard, off; and some of the* SERVANTS *bustle about, moving the table, and putting the fruit, wine, and clean drinking-vessels on it, while others turse up the skin mat, and remove it, with the weapons, kist, stools, and all chairs used in the previous Acts.*

When they have finished, MAJOR DOMO *claps hands; exeunt all remaining* SERVANTS; PAGE-BOYS *line up ready to render obeisance to* KING EDWARD *and his* COURT. *Exeunt the two* CHRONICLERS.

In a procession that passes through the audience, enter KING
EDWARD, QUEEN MARGARET, *the* LADY ISABELLA, *and their atten-
dant* CLERICS, LORDS *and* LADIES; SIR JOHN SEGRAVE, *Governor of
Scotland;* SIR JOHN LOVELL, *Captain of Stirling Castle; some*
SCOTS LORDS—BRUCE, COMYN, *the* EARL OF MARCH (*old, with a
black beard*), *and the* EARL OF ANGUS; TUMBLERS, JUGGLERS, *and*
LUTE-PLAYERS. *All are merrily talking and chattering. As* KING
EDWARD *and* QUEEN MARGARET *approach,* MAJOR DOMO *and*
PAGE-BOYS *bow them to their chairs of state, and* PAGE-BOYS *begin
serving wine, fruit, etc., to* KING, QUEEN *and* COURTIERS.

SEGRAVE [*to* QUEEN MARGARET]

It's good, Madame, to see the King merry tonight.

QUEEN MARGARET

Ah, Segrave, you speak our own thoughts.
We are not often merry these days.

KING EDWARD

Do you blame us, in this foul Scotch weather?
Hell would be kinder. But tonight!
Who would not be merry tonight,
This wretched war over at last? Soon
We'll be home again—save poor Segrave
Who must rule the place for us. See that
Standard fluttering o'er the ramparts,
Margaret? There is my sign of happiness—
The Leopards of England, my dear!

QUEEN MARGARET

I know, my lord. And we are all happy
With you to see it there at last.

KING EDWARD

And what do I use to wipe the filth
Off my hands?

82

The Lyon of Scotland!
A toothless lion now, with a twisted
Tail to boot—God be thanked and Saint John
Of Beverly. He heard me, did he not,
Deaf as he is? Ha! Ha! The holy rascal.
Ay, he heard me, did he not, old March?

MARCH

Ay, Your Majestie, he heard ye.

KING EDWARD

Cheer up, you dour old Scottishman!
Take some wine and join our merriment,
This great day.

MARCH

I've had sufficient, Majestie.

KING EDWARD

Then wipe that hangman frown off your face.
You and Angus should be pleased as I,
Should you not? Where is Angus?

ANGUS *approaches.*

ANGUS

Your Majestie?

KING EDWARD

Are you not joyous
With us today, Angus? I'd think you
At a funeral with those long looks.
By the Rood, you are too! At Scotland's
Funeral! But that should please you too,
Should it not? 'Tis part your doing,
After all.

ANGUS

Sire?

KING EDWARD

Devil take you, man!
This is your victory too, is it not?
You opened the first gate on the road,
You and March between you, at Falkirk,
That led on to Stirling and all Scotland.
Ay, Angus, you should be merry; you helped
To snuff the star that once was Wallace—
Once! Where is he now? Not in France.
We scotched that little escapade. Ah, Blackbeard,
I need traitors as a sick man physic—
And, praise be, Scotland's no dearth of them!

MARCH

Your Majestie, I beg ye—

KING EDWARD

Apologies,
My lord, but I commend you. Without
Your loyal intervention I might well be sitting
In Westminster Hall planning, with much
Inconvenience, yet another
Campaign to this forsaken wilderness.
As it is, good friend—*me voici!*
Veni, vidi, vici! Stirling is mine!
Every stronghold in Scotland is mine.
Every lord in Scotland does me homage,
Do they not, my lord?

MARCH

Ay, 'tis true,
Your Majestie, 'tis true indeed.

KING EDWARD

Do you wonder, then, I thank you for your part?
See them ranged about me at my triumph:
Bruce, Comyn, Fraser, Wishart, Ross,
Every magnate, every precious Guardian—

ANGUS

But ane, sire.

SEGRAVE

Unwise, my lord.

KING EDWARD

Speak not that name!
Remind me not of that evil broken man.
No, he is not here—but I am merry tonight,
I will not hear his name spoken. My lord,
You spoil our mood, go to and speak
With your friends.   I'll not hear that name!

ANGUS [retiring]

Your Majestie commands.

KING EDWARD

I do indeed.
Command you all.

QUEEN MARGARET

My lord, do not
Distress yourself. This is a night
Of joy and triumph.   A cup of wine
With Lady Isabella.   Child, come speak
With the King.

ISABELLA

My lord?

                    Ah, my dear,
I like a pretty face before me,
And the Queen's, alas, is not what it was.
Ha! Ha! Though, mind you, it might be
Very much worse, ha, ha!

ISABELLA

                    My lord is merry,
But unjust to the Queen—

KING EDWARD

                    Not unjust,
My dear. I but jest. I am in the mood
For jesting. But not unjust. Edward
Is never unjust, in war or peace.
Is he, old March? Would you call me unjust?

MARCH

Sire?

KING EDWARD

Have you any complaints of my justice,
Patrick?

MARCH

    I, your Majestie?

KING EDWARD

You, you egg! Is there another Patrick
Earl of March present? You were well
Rewarded, were you not, my Captain of Berwick?
The labourer is worthy of his hire,
The informer of his pay. You were well
Paid, Blackbeard, were you not? Do you complain
Of Edward's justice in the matter?

MARCH

Your Majestie, I beg to be excusit.
The heat, the noise, I dinna feel juist—

Exit MARCH.

KING EDWARD

Certainly, my lord. Go weep your guilty
Tears. But you were well paid. I insist
You *were* well paid—

QUEEN MARGARET

        My lord, restrain yourself,
You will do yourself an injury.

KING EDWARD

—Ay, well paid for Falkirk. Hollow
Victory, indeed! The sweet fruits
Snatched from my hand. Victory in the field
But a starving host and no sooner
Home than once again rebellion
Rears its shaggy head, howling for blood.
Four, five expeditions, and five conquests,
This the sixth, I've made upon these cursed
Scots. Let this be the last; I'm old
For fighting now. But will it be so?
Eh? Is it?

QUEEN MARGARET

My lord, be still. Isabella—

SEGRAVE

Ay, Your Majesty. This is the final
Conquest. Scotland is prostrate before you.

What is this Scotland?   Why does it elude me?
Her armies conquered, her strengths taken,
Her king in exile and her nobles tamed,
And one man at large!   One man!
Segrave, he must be taken.   This war must end.
I must complete what we began in Wales
And leave the State secure for the Prince.
I fear he is not strong as I;
The basis must be firm or the edifice fall.

SEGRAVE

You have made it firm, Majesty.

KING EDWARD

                              Not yet, Segrave.

ISABELLA

Prince Edward promised to be with us;
Have you heard aught from him, my lord?

KING EDWARD

Alas, my dear, the Prince
Has little love for camp or field, the clash
Of arms has little music for his ears.
But lute and viol and his peacock friends,
Consume his time with idleness and vanities.
He should be here to share our victory.
See why I must make firm the base—alas—

QUEEN MARGARET

Edward is young, my lord, and frivolous;
That is the way of youth—

KING EDWARD

Not of mine!

QUEEN MARGARET

But he is your blood, and years will bring him
Wisdom, never fear.   His heart is loving
And he is much indulged; judge him not
Too harshly.   He has time—

KING EDWARD

Which I have not.   I have no time.
Death creeps upon me every hour;
I feel him at my back—his breath is cold—
And there is much yet to be done.

QUEEN MARGARET

What talk is this, old dotard?   My Lord
Has many years ahead of strength
And peace in his achievement.
What prince in Europe has achieved so much?

KING EDWARD

Not yet, my dear.   Oh, I know well;
I am old in war and government;
And I say—and mark me, Segrave—strength
Is consolidation.   Till Britain
Is one realm her greatness cannot flower.
Scotland must succumb like Wales, or ever be
An open door to disaffection
And our enemies.   That door is not yet shut
And one man keeps it on the jar, a breach,
And mole-like mines my whole security.
One single man!   He must be taken.
He or I must die!   Scotland or England.

My lord, think not of him!
This is your final triumph here! Come now,
Enjoy what you have so boldly gained,
Old warrior.

KING EDWARD

    What is this?
What have I gained?   A devastated
Country and a restive people!
This is no peace, no victory!
What are these Scottish lords I have
At my court and entered in my peace?
Methinks they do not rule their countrymen,
But in this barren land the people rule
The lords. I have the lords! All of them!
Not one is left that has not paid
His fealty for himself, his lands,
His people. But these people—!
I have not them in my peace. A terrible
People, uncouth and sullen, owing
Allegiance to none but themselves—
And Wallace! That execrated brigand,
Devil! While he lives there is no peace
For Edward. One of us must die.
I must have Wallace. Comyn!

COMYN

Sire?

KING EDWARD

Did I not require you and some others,
On forfeit of our pleasure, to fetch me
Wallace?

COMYN

Your Majestie, I could promise
Ye nocht, and ye'll mynd nae promises
Were made. I said I'd ettle to find out
Whar his retreat micht be, and sae I've dune
And hae nocht to tell ye. He has nae force;
His guid fieres the Graham, Stewart, and MacDuff,
All fell on Fawkirk field. He is alane.
He lives in weem and forest, muves at will
And at lairge about the land. All doors
Are open for him; he bydes but a nicht,
Twa days, a week, and is awa. Nane kens whidder.
Wallace is a huntit beast—but weill-beluvit.
Nae man can kep him and nane will betray—

KING EDWARD

What, in Scotland? Are my rewards not
Great enough? Is not three hundred marks
A fortune? Is not a knighthood, lands?
Is not free pardon? What more must I offer?
Bruce, you have done us some service here
At Stirling siege; is this the limit
Of your love for us?

BRUCE

Sire, I can gie
Ye this news. Ye freed Sir Rauf de Haliburton
And sent him furth wi gowd and promises—

KING EDWARD

I did indeed. He has my authority,
Nay, my commission, to find me one to take,
I care not how, that bloody-handed man—that . . .
To find some private enemy that ill-wishes
Him and so bring him to me—

BRUCE

       Sire, I'm tauld
Sir Rauf is expectit, wi a friend, the nicht.

KING EDWARD

Ah! Bruce, this is news indeed. I thought
There must be some among the Scottish lords
That upstart had wronged. I hear—is he not
Of overbearing stomach and contempt
Towards the magnates? I could well
Believe it. Is it so?

BRUCE

      Ay, Your Majestie,
There is some deal o' truth in what ye say—

COMYN

The truth is, Majestie, the lords are laith,
Bruce is laith—dinna glower at me, my lord—

BRUCE

I'll glower when I will. And time will tell,
Comyn, whilk is the laither o' the twa o's.

          BRUCE *moves apart.*

KING EDWARD

You have angered him, Comyn. There is small
Love lost among your Scottish lords.
I would not have it otherwise, by God!
—For military reasons, if for no other.
But pray proceed, you stir me vastly.
Wallace, you were saying, the traitor—

Wallace may be traitor, as ye say;
But he is a man o' micht, sire.
We can haud him in despite, as lawlie born,
But we fear him.   You can hate him
As an enemy, but maun reckon wi'm.
Tho' defeatit, outcast, outlawed, broken,
He is aye a man o' pouer.   What he did aince,
He could weill dae again.   May I mynd
Your Majestie, wi respect, that Wallace's
Condition nou is no sae muckle unlike
What it was ere Stirling Brig was focht—

KING EDWARD

And may I remind you, Sir John de Comyn,
That I am neither Cressingham nor Surrey,
Neither was I in command nor even present
At that botched encounter on the Bridge.
Now that I am in command, Sir John,
Behold me here   Both Stirling Bridge
And Stirling town is mine, and my leopards
Float o'er Stirling Castle too!   The key that locks
The Kingdom safely in my sleeve.   Admit,
Sir John, the case is somewhat altered—

COMYN

Ay, certies, there is that, Majestie.

KING EDWARD

Good.   So we agree.   Some wine, Comyn,
To this accord continuing between us!
It gives me pleasure to have peace
At last within my grasp.
This war has been too long—and too
Expensive too.   Scotland has drained

My treasury; she owes me reparation,
Comyn, and my price—is the head of—

QUEEN MARGARET [*quickly*]

Here, my lord! Let Isabella
Serve you wine, now you are merry again,
And keep you merry—

KING EDWARD

My dear, how tactful!
Comyn, let us drink then, to accord
And our mutual interest in the matter
Of—shall we say?—a head. How's that?

COMYN

Your Majestie's servant.

KING EDWARD

Let us
Be merry and make sport. Ah yes—

Trumpet.

MAJOR DOMO

Your Majesty, His Royal Highness . . .

QUEEN MARGARET [*to* ISABELLA]

Isabella, the Prince is come—

MAJOR DOMO

. . . Edward, Prince of Wales . . . .

Enter, mincing, EDWARD PRINCE OF WALES, *with some dandified callants.*

PRINCE OF WALES

My lord, I made the best speed possible.
What country!

KING EDWARD

          Come, son, your timing is most
Happy. Go kiss the Queen, and sit you
By Isabella, who has been pining—
We have some sport afoot.

PRINCE OF WALES

Madame, apologies. And Isabella—

QUEEN MARGARET

Come, Edward—

ISABELLA

          We had thought some ill
Might have befallen you. Sit by me,
My lord. Some wine—

PRINCE OF WALES

          To be sure, yes.
And, father, I must take note of what I see,
The Leopards over Stirling! We've had
No news of this. This is cause
For merriment indeed! Now, at last!
This dull war ended—

KING EDWARD
          Maybe—

ISABELLA

You see, we celebrate in style, Edward.
And your father has some sport for us—
Have you not, my lord? You said—

KING EDWARD

I was forgetting, child. I promised you.
Son, you are most opportune. Your coming

Put it from my mind. Ladies, for this
Auspicious night I have a rare show for you,
An innocent but comical diversion
To bring sparkle to the eye and laughter
To the lip. Lovell, I think the moment
Is just ripe—

LOVELL

Sire.

KING EDWARD

Sir John de Lovell,
As new governor of Stirling Castle,
It is your duty to govern this next
Little scene. Margaret, my dear,
And Isabella too, you and your ladies
Especially, I hope, will savour this.
Are we ready, Sir John?

LOVELL

Your Majesty is sure you wish
This sport to proceed—?

KING EDWARD

I mistake
Your meaning, Sir John.

LOVELL

I wondered if Your Majesty—

KING EDWARD

Lovell, are you my Captain of Stirling?

LOVELL

Sire—

KING EDWARD
Cease then to wonder at duty.
Like fortune it could change in a wink—
My will does not, however. I asked
You, Sir John, I think, if all was ready?
Must I ask again?

LOVELL
Sir, I believe
All is ready.

KING EDWARD
Kindly proceed.

LOVELL *gives a sign, and the* MAJOR DOMO *dunts his wand of office on the floor for silence. Exeunt* JUGGLERS *and others.*

PRINCE OF WALES
What is this, my lord? Isabella,
More wine. Bear-baiting, is it?
I hope not.

KING EDWARD
You will see—It is
Something quite new, of my own devising—

PRINCE OF WALES
There is nothing new but blood
And more blood. That sickens me—

MAJOR DOMO
Pray silence, my lords, ladies and gentlemen.

Pause.

PRINCE OF WALES
Must we be silent for our sport?

Sh!

KING EDWARD

Continue, Sir John.

LOVELL

　　　　　Your Majesties,
Your Royal Highness, my lords, ladies
And gentlemen, in celebration
Of the surrender of Stirling Castle,
The last strength defying our arms
In Scotland, I have the honour
To present to the clemency
And mercy of His Majesty the King,
The former Captain of the fortress,
Sir William Oliphant and his gallant
Comrades in arms—

KING EDWARD

　　　　　　　Who have so impertinently
Denied their sovereign lord the King
Just and rightful access to this citadel
For three whole months and more—
A handful of a hundred and fifty
Starved wretches defying their liege lord,
To his unconscionable expense
Of time, energy, and gold,
By the Devil, in reducing them.
Never—

QUEEN MARGARET

　　　My lord, my lord,
Be not so hot upon them.　Calm yourself.
These men were but soldiers like yourself.

Rebels! You shall see what they are now,
My dear. Lovell, proceed with our
Entertainment.

LOVELL *signs again, the* MAJOR DOMO *raps his wand, and, through
audience, enter* SIR WILLIAM OLIPHANT, SIR WILLIAM DE DUPPLIN,
*and a dozen other gentlemen, in their shirts, barefoot, bareheaded,
chained, with ropes round their necks, escorted by* GUARDS *and two*
EXECUTIONERS, *black-masked, with long whips. There is an
audible gasp. The* LADIES *cover their faces. Some giggle. The*
PRISONERS *stand with bowed heads in their shame.*

KING EDWARD

Sir William Oliphant, Sir William
De Dupplin, you are come in strange shape.
Ha, ha! Are they not pretty, ladies?
[*To* QUEEN] My dear, are they not pretty men?

QUEEN MARGARET

Send them away, my lord. Send them away!
This should not be!

KING EDWARD

                    Gentlemen, you are forgetting
Your bond. To save those pretty heads
You must kneel and beg the royal clemency.

They bide standing.

Kneel, I say!

Some kneel.

SIR WILLIAM OLIPHANT [*standing*]
Sire, this is owre muckle.

KING EDWARD

I have your wife, Sir William, I would

99

Remind you.   And some also of these
Other knights.   Kneel!

Pause.   Then they kneel.

There, that is better.
Now you may go, but first, pray you
To walk round once, so that the ladies
Can view you better, and from behind, ha, ha!

MAJOR DOMO *raps wand.   They rise and walk round.*

Yes, yes, a pretty sight, to be sure!
Are they not, ladies?

QUEEN MARGARET

My lord, send them away—

LOVELL [*to* SEGRAVE, *apart*]

This is unseemly, Segrave.
I would not for the world have witnessed this.

SEGRAVE

Wallace has turned his head.
We must take that man, and soon. . . .
This is nigh to madness, Lovell.

QUEEN MARGARET

Enough, my lord, I pray you, enough!
My ladies are distresst.   Dismiss them,
Sir John, I pray you!

KING EDWARD

No, no, not yet.   We have not seen them dance.
Revolve, gentlemen!   Round again!   Can
You not dance a little?   Dance, I say—!

My lord, my lord—

KING EDWARD

> No, they shall dance!
Use your whips, villains! Dance!

They are whipt.

Ha, ha! That's better far! Lay on! Lay on!

Ladies scream.

Ha, ha! What did your Wallace say?
Hop if you can!

Whips.

> Lay on, villains,
Or answer for it! Well, you are
In the ring again; hop, sirs, if you will!
Ha, ha, ha! Ha, ha, ha! Well done, well done!
Lay on, my hearties! Lay on!

QUEEN MARGARET [*hammering on* EDWARD'S *shoulder*]

My lord, stop this, stop this, I pray you!
My ladies—

PRINCE OF WALES [*on his feet, staring*]

> Blood, blood!
There is never enough blood!

> *He runs hysterically out.*

KING EDWARD

What ails the Prince? His lily liver?
These are Scots and must be broken. Alas,
He has no stomach for the act and must
Be taught his part—

My lord, my lord, I pray you—
Isabella, go to the Prince—

ISABELLA [*sobbing*]

Yes, ma'am.

Exit ISABELLA.

KING EDWARD

Very well, my dear, since you insist—
And Edward's chicken heart—ah, well—
But it was a pleasant sight, surely.

He claps hands.

Gentlemen, your sport is at an end.
We thank you, but the Queen's mercy
Bids you cease your capering. Lovell,
See them returned to their dungeons.
Look your last on Scotland, sirs,
For many a summer. Adieu!

Exeunt PRISONERS, GUARDS *and* EXECUTIONERS.

My lords,
You may report this joyous spectacle
To your Wallace, I would have you do so
And to tell him we shall make him dance
As well, but to a yet livelier tune.
Eh, Comyn?

COMYN

Ye maun kep your maukin
Or ye cook him, Majestie.

KING EDWARD

I shall " kep " him, Comyn.
If I don't, or if you don't, my lords,

Ere Christmas, I could, and will retract
The concessions of your peace.   Our
Interests are common in this matter.
Be advised—

Enter ISABELLA.

                Ah, here is little
Isabella back from the sick-room—

ISABELLA

My lord.

QUEEN MARGARET

How is the prince, child?

ISABELLA

He would not open to me, ma'am.
And he would not come out, neither.
He has his friends with him—I know not. . . .

KING EDWARD

Ah, let him be.   He has his own pleasures.
They are not mine, *pardie*, but then
Mine are not his—so we are quits!
Ha! Ha! But you look pale, my dear.
Some wine will bring the roses back—

MAJOR DOMO

Your Majesty—

KING EDWARD

What then?

MAJOR DOMO

Sire, Sir Ralph de Haliburton.
He is with another—

> Aha! At last.

Bid them approach instanter.

> MAJOR DOMO *bows.* *Exit.*

A pity they were not earlier!
Now, Comyn, we shall see whether God
Has delivered my malkin into my hands
For cooking.

Enter MAJOR DOMO *with* SIR RALPH DE HALIBURTON *and* SIR JOHN
MENTEITH.

> Gentlemen, you are most welcome.

Alas, you have just missed a splendid show.
A thousand pities. But pray approach.
Sir Ralph, you find us merry tonight.
I hope you will make us merrier.

HALIBURTON

Your Majestie. I hae the honour
To present Sir John Menteith, that bears
Luve til your Majestie and hatred
Til your enemies.

MENTEITH [*bowing*]
Sire.

KING EDWARD

> My condolences,

Sir John. I'm told your nephew Sir John
Stewart of Bonkill died heroically
On Falkirk field.

MENTEITH
That is true, sire.

KING EDWARD

He chose the wrong side, Menteith.

MENTEITH

That, tae, is true, Your Majestie.

KING EDWARD

You have some news for us? Of Wallace?
You have seen him? You can take him?

MENTEITH

Sire, on this maitter I hae thocht some deal.
It is nae semple gait. My past nichts
Hae seen smaa sleep, warslin back and furth,
Seekin whar my dutie led and whar
My private wish; whilk road lay Scotland's
Honour and whilk her weill-being—

KING EDWARD

I have simple answers to all these,
Sir John.

MENTEITH

      I hae nae dout, Majestie.
But I maun answer for mysel,
And tae mysel, in this.

KING EDWARD

      Yes, yes,
I see that. Pray continue, Sir John.

MENTEITH

Wallace has lichtlied me, as maybe
Ye ken, Majestie, and my young nephew,
That I loed fu weill, is deid for Wallace's
Vainglorie. Sic things canna be forgot.

Indeed, Sir John.   It touches honour.

MENTEITH

But there is the general skaith as weill
That touches aa.   Scotland wants peace
And comitie—this landless brag
Divides us wi his wilyart pride,
Sets men agane their lords wi's vain
Imaginings and nou fructless strife.
The war is endit, but there is nae peace—

KING EDWARD

My very words, Sir John.   But to the point,
My friend.   I see your drift.   What then?
Keep me not dangling more, I pray you.
Can he be taken?

MENTEITH

                    Sire, I like nocht
The errand I am on, but I like
Wallace less—and peace mair.
The roads aa lead the ae airt.
Ay, he can be taen, but no eithlie.

KING EDWARD

Ah, that is better, friend.   Your motives
Are to me as chaff, your acts as wine
And honey.   Wallace, our tracks begin to meet,
Our fates entwine like deadly lovers'.
We are drawing together, you and I,
And it will be on my terms that we join.
Tell me more, Menteith, I am on fire.

MENTEITH

This is no for aabodie's lugs, Your Majestie.

KING EDWARD

We all know your purpose here, Sir John.
Many a Scottish lord would take your place,
If he could, or if he dared.

MENTEITH

This is no for ithers, Majestie.

KING EDWARD [*leading him apart*]

As you will, friend.   We are alone.

BRUCE [*to* COMYN, *aside*]

I dinna like the stink o' this, Comyn.
Can ye get word to Wallace?

COMYN

Let things be as they will be;
We can dae nocht.

BRUCE

I wad get word til him.

Exit BRUCE.

MENTEITH

Wallace is a Will-o-the-mist.
Nae man can tell whar he will be
Or when.   But aa men are his friends . . .
And aa wemen.

KING EDWARD

I smell a trace.

MENTEITH

He has a leman, Ailish Rae,
That has a drucken brither wi nae luve
For Wallace.

That is very foolish
Of our man, and most fortunate for us.
The world is full of women, but a drunkard's
Mouth has no door. But you, Menteith—
He will suspect you, surely—

MENTEITH

Though I hate him, sire, I haena tint
His confidence—

KING EDWARD

But you deserted him—
Say rather, you withdrew from him, Sir John,
You and Comyn, at Falkirk field, did you not?

MENTEITH

I never gied him promise o' support,
I never focht agane him. He has
Nae wide reason to fear me. Nane.
Sire, wad ye treat wi him?

KING EDWARD *and* MENTEITH *return to the company and speak
at large.*

KING EDWARD

Treat with Wallace? Never! Wallace
Is exempt from treaty, expressly
By my public writ. I will treat with him
No more than he with me. We two are ranged
Implacably; our feud is to the death.
Never shall I, can I, grant honour
To a brigand, traitor, reptile, to this
Scorning fiend, this wolf, this—

QUEEN MARGARET

My lord, sit back. Quietly, Sir John.
Sir Ralph, the King is quickly roused,

It is not well to anger him.   My lord,
Be easy.   Talk of this tomorrow—

KING EDWARD

Woman, desist.   This is man's talk.
Menteith, I am old; my days are numbered.
Margaret, when I die, I would have you
Tell the Prince, if ever he have trouble
With these Scots, to bear my bones
Before his army as palladium.
I would wish to be present ever
In a war with Wallace's kin.   I would—

QUEEN MARGARET

A grim jest, my lord.

KING EDWARD

Ah, no, indeed.   I joot not, my dear.
The bones of saints have worked their wonders
For the pious; who can say perhaps
A soldier's bones have virtue for the warlike?
No, no, Menteith.   No treaty.   There is
Nothing for it but my death or his; and
He is youthful—I cannot wait for him
To die.   Time is for him, not me.
You say it will be difficult to take him.
—Then take him not but kill him.
Ah, but rather take him and bring him to me.
I must be sure.   But you must be soon.
Tell me your price, Menteith.
I might not live another winter.
Wallace is a gadfly.   Stirling Bridge
Was more victory for him than Falkirk
Was for me.   At Stirling he gained Scotland;

At Falkirk I did not win it.
His armies rise like grass
From the earth, the very stones, of Scotland.
He is a sorcerer, a devil!

QUEEN MARGARET

My lord, my lord—

KING EDWARD

        Now, Scotland is at peace—
All but this one man. And lo, I am not
At peace! Nor can be while Wallace lives—

MENTEITH

Gif onie man can get him, I sall get him.

KING EDWARD

Go then, Menteith! Do what you have to do
And do it quickly. Take what you need
From my Treasurer—and the Lord
Have mercy on your soul. I do not envy
You your enterprise, nor the fairy gold
Of your success. But it must be done,
And for him who does it there's no limit
To my bounty and my love. Three hundred,
Nay, three thousand marks, and the lordship
Of wide Lennox. Are you for the price,
Menteith?

MENTEITH

       As ye say, Majestie. But . . .
It's no for the gowd nor yet the lordship
I dae this but the rebuke he's pitten
On my house, and peace for this herriet land
I dae't.

Go then. With my blessing.

MENTEITH

Your Majestie's servant.

As MENTEITH *turns to leave, the* SCOTS LORDS *turn their backs upon him in silence.*

My lords, it's weill for ye to turn your backs
Sae we canna see the shame upon your fronts.
Nae lord here but wishes Wallace deid;
Nae lord here that hasna bent his knee til the King
And begged his clemencie; nane but envies
Me the King's largesse—but nane has courage
For the deed I dae. Ilkane here wad liefer
Keep his lands in servitude nor loss them
For Scotland free. Weill ye may
Turn your backs, my lords—and bless me
When I'm gane! I am your scapegoat here
And weill ye ken it. But I bring Scotland
Peace at last. Guidnicht!

Exit MENTEITH. *Pause.* SCOTS LORDS *turn slowly back and look at one another.*

KING EDWARD

Menteith has said the word. Goodnight.
Goodnight, my lords, ladies. Pray for the soul
Of Sir John Menteith. Come, madam.

QUEEN MARGARET

Poor man!

KING EDWARD

I would not be that man
Or his son or his son's son

III

For the crown of Charlemagne itself
And all the gold in Christendom.

Exeunt KING *and* QUEEN, *followed by* COURTIERS.

Directed by MAJOR DOMO, PAGE-BOYS *and* COURT SERVANTS *remove hangings, clear away all fruit, wine, drinking-vessels, etc., and finally remove all furniture, leaving the stage bare.*

There follows an INTERVAL.

ACT IV

A POOR COTTAGE IN THE WOODS
ROBROYSTON

5 August 1305

A stormy night. In a dim licht, enter the two CHRONICLERS, *followed and assisted by* DONALD, *and carrying a rough wooden kist, skins, stools, coarse thick candles stuck in square wooden candlesticks, weapons, and the Bluidie Clout. Whiles speaking, whiles working, they set the scene. When they have finished,* DONALD *sets up the Bluidie Clout.*

ENGLISH CHRONICLER

Turn we now other ways and speak of the Wallace that lies in the forest, hunted and alone, who continued to defy the King. It was the King's will that three hundred marks should be their reward, whoever should take this traitor or bring his head to London.

SCOTS CHRONICLER

Some wheen of his friends socht to prevail upon the Wallace to come intil King Edward's peace, as had all the ither great men in Scotland—but until them he replied: " Gif the haill folk of Scotland should yield obedience til the King of England, I and my fieres that cleave til me will aye stand for the libertie of the Kingrik or daith sall free us frae this trewage. And with God's aid we sall obey nae ither man but the crounit King of Scots or him that's acting in his name by his authoritie. Tak ye thir words til Edward, and bring nae answer back, but a sword."

ENGLISH CHRONICLER

They say he lives with savages and evil-doers in moors and marshes and feeds himself with robbery.

SCOTS CHRONICLER

He bydes at Rob Rae's toun, a puir rouch bield in the wuids by Glasgow, he and his fair leman, that never left his side. . . .

Exeunt the CHRONICLERS.

Enter AILISH RAE *and* WALLACE, *in dripping cloaks, which they fling off and give to* DONALD.

WALLACE

Ech, what a nicht! Nae weather for a dug!
Some yill, Donald, save us! Nae news?

DONALD [*taking cloaks*]

My leddie. No, Sir Weelum.

AILISH

Be thankit, Donald.

DONALD [*getting ale and horn mugs from back*]

Ay, it's a coorse nicht. This'll cheer ye.

AILISH *gets a small lute from back, sits down on a stool, and croons owre a wee tune, while* WALLACE *pours ale.*

WALLACE

Ailish, to your bonnie blue ee!
And bless the day ye cam til me!
Hear yon? Ye've made me a bard!
Naebodie ever did yon afore.

AILISH

Will!

Dinna stap your singin, lass.
It's as bonnie as you, and ah,
It mynds me o' the day—lang syne—
Hou lang?—

AILISH

Five year, Will, it's nou, sen . . .
Rob's ne'er forgien us.

WALLACE

Never heed Rob.
A brither's nae richt o' his sister,
Onieweys—that I ever heard.

AILISH

He'd like us to be mairrit, though—
Ach, weill!

WALLACE

" Ach, weill " is richt.
And the bairn's sauf in France.
Dinna stap singin, lass. I'm juist
Bletherin awa til mysel, like an auld
Carle, o' blyther days.

AILISH

I'm blyth, luve—

WALLACE

Ay, but ye're a wonderfu woman,
Wi nocht in your mynd but luve—

AILISH

Times'll cheynge, Will. They canna
Ding my Wallace doun for aye—

Yon's the sperit! Mair yill, Ailie!
Donald! . . .

DONALD *gets ale.*

        Times'll cheynge. . . . Ay, they'll cheynge
And for the better, tae. They
Couldna get waur.

DONALD *pours ale.*

AILISH

        Be thankit, Donald.
Hae a drap t'yoursel.

DONALD

        Ay, my leddie.
A stoup's grand for the bluid

Storm.

On a nicht like this.

WALLACE

Nae sign o' Rob?

DONALD

        Na hint na hair o' the man.

WALLACE

Whar in the Deil's name's he gotten til?
Twa days and nichts at Glesca Fair's
A day and a nicht owre monie thae days.
He'll be richt eneuch gin he doesna
Get fechtin. . . . Men at my back!

DONALD

I'll awa out and hae a glisk around.

WALLACE

Ay, Donald.

Exit DONALD. *Storm.*

AILISH

Och, Will, ye dinna think—?

WALLACE

Na, na, lassie. Juist bletherin.
I'm cantie the nicht, for the morn's
The day micht cheynge aa.

AILISH

     Ye're no gaun, Will?
Dinna gang!

WALLACE

   Ay, I maun gang.
And I want Rob here, to be wi ye.
I'll need Donald for mysel.
Men at my back, ay! Yon's the haill airmie
O' Wallace nou! But no for lang!

AILISH

Will, dinna gang. Can Bruce no come here?

WALLACE

Daft lassie! D'ye think the plain
Sir William Wallace, outlaw, can demand
O' Robert Bruce, Earl o' Carrick and Lord
Of Annandale, to dance attendance
At his pleisure and present his sel
At a clay biggin in the wuids at a word?
As Guairdian o' Scotland, I could ettle,
Maybe, and hope for the best—

117

As a huntit outlaw, huntit e'en
By the noble lords o' Scotland—?
Think again, Ailie.

Storm: distant thunder.

AILISH

I fear for ye, Will.

WALLACE

      Na, I maun gang.
I canna put bye the chance; and it was
Trystit langsyne. I maun meet
The Bruce. It's the chance could cheynge
The haill war. Sen Stirling fell wi Oliphant,
Edward weirs aa Scotland like a raggit
Robe. For what it is, 'tis aa his.
Aa the lords, and Bruce amang them, ilka
Baron in the realm is in his peace!
But me! And I'm nae baron. Their pride
Is doun sae laich they draw thegither
In their ignominie. They murmur.
Bruce and Comyn has been in truce
Or this, and could be again.
Ay, tyke wi swine drink the waters o'
Tribulation thegither, and thegither
They could turn and rend the hand that feeds
Them nocht but shame, humiliation
And dishonour. The folk thole it
For they're used wi't. But the lords are humbelt.
They wreathe and thraw. They want a cleg to stang
Their pride til action and aa could cheynge
In a nicht. And, Ailie, [*smiling*] it's me, I think,
'S the cleg. They hae nae luve for me, I ken;
But I've nae choice. Scotland's groans
Dirl in my heid like drums. I maun see Bruce
The morn.

But Will, my ain Will,
Ye've enemies on ilka road.
Hae ye nae fear o' traitorie?
Ah, the wind hears me! Hark til
Its warnin, Wallace!

WALLACE

Havers, lassie!
The Sudron hears the same wind.
Its warnin is for him.

AILISH

But the King's
Set a fortune on your heid.
Three hunder merks is riches, Will,
And sair temptation. Dinna gang til Bruce!
For my sake, Will, for our luve's sake,
Dinna gang!

WALLACE

Traitorie
Frae Bruce, ye mean?

AILISH

Frae onie!

WALLACE

Frae nane! Bruce is to be King. I'm nae
Rival there, for aa they say. Wad ye like
Wallace a king?

AILISH

Never! It wadna
Dae for us—and Wallace is king
Eneuch for me as it is. But, Will—
There's ithers but Bruce that loe ye nocht.

Lassie, d'ye no see? Though nane o' the lords
Is for me, they never were; naething's
Cheyngit. It was aye the Donalds
And the Robs o' Scotland were my fieres,
The plain folk wi scant an acre
Til their name but luve for it aa.
Thir were aa my companie—but the few
Like Murray and Graham, aa gane nou
Til their warrior's rest—God sain
Their noble sauls!

He drinks.

AILISH

I never kent but Donald.

WALLACE

Aa gane, aa deid, and guid MacDuff.
Their bluid has riched the Scottish earth, be-God,
And whar they fell the mools is routh
Wi heroes. Rich and fowthie. Ay,
Giants will breed frae't. Na, na, lass,
Though nane o' the lords is for me, nane's
Agane me. Though I count my force on ae
Hand wi ease, I fear nae traitorie—
I ken weill eneuch they fear my vengeance
Gin they miss their mark. Aa men has heard
Of Heselrig. They ken o' the Barns
Of Ayr. They ken the fate o' Cressingham.
Na, na. . . .

AILISH

I fear traitorie, Wallace.
I loe ye weill; I feel sauf in your airms,
But when I'm no, when you're awa,

I feel huntit here; enemies
At ilka tree. I suspicion aa.
Whar's Donald nou? Whar's Rob? E'en my ain
Brither! I feel traitorie as the air
About me, as a beast feels
Lang or the tempest cracks—

Crack of thunder. Pause.

Like yon!

WALLACE

Lassie-luve, this is idle freits
And fancies. I'll to Bruce the morn,
And when I'm back all haill and sauf
Will ye be aisie then, and say maybe
Your Wallace kens mair o' the maitter
Nor Ailish does, for aa her woman's fore-sicht?
Hae some yill and gie's a sang, sweet Ailie.
And forget aa eeriness.

AILISH

I sall be aisie,
Ah my hairt, when aa this is endit
And at peace and Wallace content at last—

She fingers the strings of her lute and sings the first few lines of her song:

Alane in langour as I lay
Underneath a seemlie tree,
Saw I whare a ladye gay
Cam ridin owre a lang lee.

Her palfry was a dapple gray
Sic as I never saw me nane,
As does the sun on simmer day
Yon fair ladye her sel did sheen.

But I speak with yon ladye bricht,
I hope my hairt will brist in three;
Nou sall I gang with all my micht
Her to meet at Eildon Tree.

There nou, does yon content ye?

WALLACE

Wallace will hae content wi Scotland free
And no afore, luve.   And no till then—
Nae ither road—

AILISH

No juist wi me?

WALLACE

Ailie, without ye, thae last years,
I micht hae tint aa hope.   Mirren gane,
Murray gane, Graham—the leet is lang.
Fawkirk battle lost.   Reject
By the lords, the Guairdianship
Put bye.   I micht hae tint aa hope.

AILISH

What-like was Mirren, Will?
Ye never speak o' her.

WALLACE

She was bonnie, Ailie.
Like you.   It's monie a year nou.
Scotland became my luve and she Scotland.
Scotland is like a bonnie woman pent
Ahint castle waas.   The castle maun be
Forced and she deliverit frae her bands—
And Ailie, dearie, our luve's in prison tae,
Just as was Mirren's langsinsyne.

No for me, Will. I said I felt huntit,
But we're free yet. They haena taen us yet.
Wi you, aawhar is freedom, luve.
For you are libertie itsel.
You yoursel is freedom, Will.

WALLACE

And you are luve, Ailie. As Scotland
Is, and freedom tae. Freedom is nae
Place set apairt; like tyrannie
It's neutral. Aa men in chains the day
Are Scots and Scotland the world o' slaves
And prisoners. Juist as you, Ailie lass,
Are luve and freedom huntit in this wuid,
Sae ye are Scotland tae [*storm*], and Scotland
Freedom—ach, I hae nae words
For what I mean. . . .

AILISH

I am thy luve,
Will, and will be for ever.

WALLACE

Gin they let us.

Torches, clatter, voices, off. WALLACE *starts up, sword in hand.*

What's this?

Enter DONALD *with* MENTEITH. *Storm.*

DONALD

Sir Weelum—It's—

WALLACE

Menteith! What means this?

I come as a friend, Wallace.   Guid e'en
T'ye, my leddie.

WALLACE [*lowering sword*]

I hae few friends, Menteith.
But gin ye speak sooth, ye're weilcome.
Set ye doun.   Donald, a stoup for Sir John.

MENTEITH *puts off wet cloak, sword, etc.*

DONALD

Ay, Sir Weelum.

MENTEITH

No for me.

WALLACE

What brings ye here
On sic a nicht, Menteith?   Hou kent ye
I was here?   Wha guidit ye?   Hou monie's
Wi ye?

MENTEITH

Mysel and twa lads.
I've a message frae the Earl
O' Carrick, Wallace.

WALLACE

So?   Donald, keep
A guid watch on the door.

DONALD

Ay, Sir Weelum,
I'll dae yon.

Exit DONALD.

124

MENTEITH

As for hou did I ken
Ye were here, tongues wag, and drucken
Tongues maist.

WALLACE

Rob Rae!

MENTEITH

Ye hae a brither,
Leddie Ailish.

AILISH

He's aaricht?

MENTEITH

He's richt eneuch.
But for some men o' mine at Glesca Fair
He'd be in an English dungeon nou.
He's weill eneuch. I had to find ye,
Wallace—Providence sent Rae.
And here I am.

WALLACE

Ye said ye'd a message.

MENTEITH

Ay, frae Bruce. Ye were to meet him
The morn's morn in Glesca. The Burgh Mair?

WALLACE

Weill?

MENTEITH

Ye canna gang.

AILISH [*relieved*]

     Oh, Sir John!

WALLACE

Says Bruce?

MENTEITH

    His sel. The English ken ye're here.
They've three-score men-at-airms comin here
At dawn to tak ye.

     Pause.

     They dinna
Undervalue ye, Wallace.

AILISH

    Will!

WALLACE [*gripping his sword*]

     Never!

MENTEITH

We maun see they dinna.

WALLACE

     Menteith,
Ye speak in riddles. Tell me aa.

MENTEITH

Bruce is at Ayr. Ye're to come wi me
And jyne him there. He's hystin the standard.

WALLACE

No! Wha's wi him?

MENTEITH

Comyn, Fraser, Wishart.
Three thousand men. They need ye. They're mairchin
On Stirling. The war is on again.
Gin ye byde here the nicht ye're dune.

WALLACE

I canna believe it.

MENTEITH

Believe or nocht, as ye will.
Ye'll see the morn.

AILISH

Oh, Will!
Hae ye letters frac Bruce, Sir John?

MENTEITH

No, my leddie, there was nae time. And there's
Nae time the nou, gin ye'd sauf your man.

WALLACE

It seems queer, and gey sudden.
But I maun tak your word, Menteith. . . .

Storm.

Ailish, ye'd better get readied.

AILISH

No!

MENTEITH

The suner the better, my leddie.
This storm'll help our passage.

Ay, it will, tae.

AILISH

I winna gang. Wallace, I beg ye—

WALLACE

Ailie, we've had aa this.
Ye ken I maun gang. Get readied, lass.

AILISH *goes reluctantly to the kist and begins packing clothes in two
leather saddle-bags.*

Sae Bruce has turnit again. And Comyn tae.
Whilk is the tyke and whilk the swine, think ye?
But weill eneuch, Menteith. Things couldna
Get waur. I felt the cheynge was comin.
Nou, at last! Nou for the final cast!

MENTEITH

Anither thing. Wallace, the kintra's
Live wi Sudron troops. Gin they see's
We canna pass them. I should say,
Gin they see you. As ye ken, I'm in Edward's
Peace. I haud Dumbarton Castle for'm.
To win through the kintra sauf, we thocht
A guid guise wad be for ye to seem
My prisoner—

WALLACE

Hou d'ye mean?

MENTEITH

It were best, we thocht, gin ye rade
Wi me as a prisoner, shachelt. Sae,
We can ride openlie wi nae fear.
They winna touch *me*.

128

WALLACE

       Menteith, dinna
Mock me, I warn ye! I'm an ill man to cross.

MENTEITH

Wallace, I speak in earnest.
This is nae time for braggandie.
Neither Wallace nor Menteith is muckle
Guid to Scotland liggin deid
In the forest or in an English
Dungeon bydin Edward's justice.
Gin we meet troops—and we canna hope
No to meet troops—what chance has twa-three men
At sic odds?

WALLACE

     I've focht through twa-three score
O' men or this, Menteith, and will again.

MENTEITH

No three score or threttie score, Wallace;
There's mair like ten thousand troops
Twix Ayr and Glesca, nou. I'm tellin
Ye the truth. I've been through them.
Maybe ye could win through, maybe indeed
Ye could. But ye'll admit that even
Wallace maybe couldna. Ye could fail—
And we canna count the possibilitie
O' failin.

WALLACE

   I couldna dream o't. Drunk
Or sober. A strang richt airm, a sword,
And a guid hairt—and gin we fail, we faa.

MENTEITH

Wallace, this is idle vanitie speakin.
Is it your ain honour and glorie ye seek—
Or Scotland's freedom?

WALLACE

D'ye see muckle
Honour and glorie here, Menteith?

MENTEITH

Div I see Scotland's freedom either?
Wallace, gin ye reject this, it's
Nocht but wilfu pride, a sin,
A sin agane honour and agane Scotland's honour.

WALLACE

Put a watch on your tongue,
Menteith.   I wad dee for Scotland blythlie,
As [*gripping sword*] Scotland kens by this, as ye can pruve
Instanter gin ye wish.

MENTEITH

We can aa dee.
I'm askin ye to live for Scotland.
To sauf your life to sauf and serve hers.
I hae shawn ye the road to that service,
Your pride humbelt to raise hers.   To pass through
The Sudron hosts as prisoner, to live
For Scotland's sake—no to dee amang them
As warrior for your ain vain glorie's,
And there an end.   Lower your pride, Wallace!
Hae mynd of Fawkirk and be humble.

WALLACE

I mynd Fawkirk aaricht, Menteith.   Dae you?

MENTEITH

I dinna forget.   I was humbelt there
For Scotland's sake—though I ken ye look
Upon it ithergates.   Can Wallace
Dae the like?

Pause.

Maybe it's owre dour for ye.
I've dune what I could.   My conscience
Is clear.   I beg my leave.   And your pairdon.

WALLACE

No sae quick, Menteith.   Ye hae some richt o't.
In battle, with owrehailin odds to face,
It's aye the wyce sodjer's dutie to draw aff
And fecht again than dee foolhardilie—
The war is worth a battle.   Ay. . . .

Pause.   Storm.

I'll dae't.   I'm wi ye, Menteith.

AILISH

Wallace, no!

WALLACE

It's a chance.   I maunna put it bye.
Ye said " shachelt."

MENTEITH

They maun *see* ye bund

WALLACE

Ay, I ken.   Ye'll need a whang, or cords—

MENTEITH

I kent your answer wad be, Wallace;
I hae airns here.

He produces manacles.

AILISH

I dinna like this, Will.

WALLACE

I like it as bonnie weill as a cat
Likes mustard.   But it's a chance, and we maun
Pree it, and let be what maun be.

He holds out his wrists.

Dae what ye maun dae, Menteith.

As MENTEITH *locks the manacles on his wrists, there is a clash of weapons, off, and, with a cry of " Treason! "* DONALD *runs in and falls mortally wounded, with several armed* TROOPERS *after him.* AILISH *screams.*

WALLACE [*misunderstanding*]

Menteith!   Til airms!

Manacled, he seizes the spear with the Bluidie Clout, and lays about him, but is stunned by a dunt on the head from behind, and falls.

MENTEITH

Dinna touch him!   I want him alive!

AILISH *falls on her knees by* WALLACE.

DONALD [*dying*]

We are betrayit!

AILISH

Will! Will!

WALLACE *stirs and comes to.*

WALLACE

Ailie! Ye're aaricht?

AILISH

Oh, Will! Will!

MENTEITH [*to* TROOPERS]

Get him til his feet!

WALLACE [*dumfounded*]

Menteith! D'ye mean—? Is this—?

WALLACE *struggles with* TROOPERS. *They pin him.*

MENTEITH

It's nae guid, Wallace. This is
Your owrehailin odds. Sauf your strenth,
Ye'll hae need o't.

WALLACE

To thraw your thrapple, caitiff!

He struggles.

MENTEITH

I dout ye'll hae pickle opportunitie,
Sir Weelum. This is the end. The house
Is surroundit wi three score men-at-airms,
Juist as I said. I tellt ye we didna
Undervalue ye.

WALLACE

Scum!

He sees DONALD.

And Donald?

AILISH [*beside* DONALD]

He's gane, Will. Oh, Will!

133

Puir Donald! Mair bluid for Scotland's sake.
When will her hunger be stecht? Bluid
And traitorie biggs her historie.
Ah, Menteith, ye vile thing!
Animal! Why did ye dae't?
Siller? Land? Hou muckle was I worth?

MENTEITH

No, Wallace, ye canna mock me nou.
Ye mockit me at Fawkirk field;
Ye put a black affront upon my house
And Stewart deed thereby. Ye killt him,
Wallace. Nane ither.

WALLACE

　　　　Stewart deed
Brawlie and honourablie for Scotland,
While you stude idle wi your chivalrie,
And Comyn tae. Gin onie killt him
But the arrow in his craig—it was you,
His uncle, and his friend, forleetin him.
Ah, Scotland, thir are aa your sons.

MENTEITH

This is for Scotland, Wallace.
Owre lang ye've been the creuk o' quarrel,
Envie and division. Ye crippled Scotland
Wi your vaunt and vanitie. Your day is dune.
Nou Scotland can embrace a doucer weird
In comitie and peace wi England
And hersel. She has her glut o' bluid.

WALLACE

Ye think her weird can e'er be in the hands
O' the likes o' you, Menteith?

Traitors and pultroons?   Think again!
Gin ever Scotland looks wi luve
And gratitude on Menteith, Scotland
Is deid wi a worm at her hairt
And isna worth reprival.   Let her dee.
Nou, Judas, finish your work
And finish swithlie!

AILISH

No!   No!   Oh, Will, no!

Sir John, I beg ye!

She kneels at MENTEITH's *feet, pleading.   He kicks her off.*

MENTEITH

Peace, hure!
Gin I'm Judas, are you Christ,
And this your Magdalene?   Wallace
Wants a muckler croun nor Scotland's,
Seeminlie.   Blasphemious infidel cur!

WALLACE

Ye use lewd langage on a waik woman,
Sir.   I admire your courage.   But eneuch
O' this and your fine speak of infidelitie.
Be faithfu at least til your enmitie.

He flings back his head.

AILISH

No, Will!   No!   No!   I beg ye!

WALLACE

Here is my halse, Menteith!   Strike!

MENTEITH

Na, na, my brave mannie.   We've a journey
Afore us.

AILISH *sobs with relief.*

Sae it wasna private
Vengeance, as ye said?   Wha sent ye, then?
Whase man are ye?

MENTEITH

Ye'll see.

WALLACE

No Bruce's?

MENTEITH

Ye'll see, I said.   Bruce kens nocht o' this.

WALLACE

Anither lee?   But what's a lee
Less or mair til sic a leear
As Menteith-*Menteur*?   Was't Comyn?
Why should it be Comyn?

MENTEITH [*flinging* WALLACE's *cloak about him*]

We dinna wish
Ye to dee for cauld on the road.
We gang nou.

WALLACE

Whar are ye takkin me,
Menteith?

MENTEITH

Come on.

WALLACE [*understanding*]

No!   Could ye sink
As laich as *that*?

No respond.

Ye did!

AILISH [*gasps*]

No!

WALLACE

Ye did! Ye did, tae!
And it took a Scot to dae't!
Ah, Edward! At last!

MENTEITH

Tak him awa!

AILISH

No, no! Oh, Will! Will!

She clings to him but is flung aside.

WALLACE

The Clout, Ailie! To gie til Edward.

WALLACE *is surrounded by* TROOPERS. AILISH *runs and rives the Bluidie Clout from its spearhead and sticks it in* WALLACE'*s belt. They hustle him out.*

AILISH

Will!

WALLACE

Ailie, fareweill, my luve. For ever.

Exeunt WALLACE *among* TROOPERS, *followed by* MENTEITH.

AILISH

Will! Will! Oh, Will!

She runs out after them, crying his name. Two TROOPERS *return, after her exit, and bear* DONALD'*s body off on a hurdle, kicking the stools out of their road as they leave. The stage is empty.*

ACT V

THE GREAT HALL
WESTMINSTER

23 August 1305

Lights up. Enter the two CHRONICLERS, *and an* ENGLISH HERALD, *followed by a host of* ARTISANS, *carrying the Royal Throne of West- minster, some benches, a table, documents, hangings, and such other appurtenances as may be needful. The* CHRONICLERS, *whiles working, whiles speaking, gather up the kist, stools, skins, etc., used in Act IV, and the* ARTISANS, *directed by the* HERALD, *put the throne on the deis at back, arrange table and benches, and (with at first a good deal of hammering) erect the dock—a platform, not so high as the King's deis, fenced round with solid wooden railings.*

SCOTS CHRONICLER

It was a lang and dowie journeying they had. The fause Menteith first took the Wallace til Dumbarton Castle, whar he was deliverit up til the English Governor of Scotland, Sir John de Segrave, that lay there to receipt him. Syne they made a muckle convoy, and all the touns they passit on the road til Carlisle had all their winnocks shut and steekit close as gin the plague was in the streets that was but noble Wallace and his companie.

ENGLISH CHRONICLER

Seventeen days they were on the road, with games and high wassail in every town they passed, through England, into

London, where great numbers of men and women thronged the streets and stood wondering upon him.

SCOTS CHRONICLER

And anither train gaed doun in Wallace's wake, of noble Scottis lords that King Edward had set in authoritie in Scotland, and thir lords he gart compear for Pairliament in London to see his justice dune that was nae justice but a court of executioners.

ENGLISH CHRONICLER

To his Treasurer the lord King Edward commanded that forty marks be given to the varlet that spied out the rebel, and sixty to the others who took part in the capture, to be divided equally among them. To Sir John Menteith for his loyal services he granted land of a hundred pounds rent and also the Earldom of Lennox and the temporalities of the Bishopric of Glasgow in the County of Dumbarton. All London wore their best that day, the Eve of St Bartholomew, in honour of a scoundrel brought to book. But hark! This is the ending of the tale, in Great Westminster Hall....

Distant fanfare. Exeunt the CHRONICLERS, *and all* ARTISANS, *taking the kist, stools, skins, etc., used in Act IV.*

Enter, through audience, MEN-AT-ARMS, *followed by* MINOR CLERICS, CLERKS OF COURT, SIR GEOFFREY DE HARTLEPOOL, LORDS *and* GENTLEMEN. *All bow gravely to the* HERALD, *and take their places. Fanfare.*

HERALD

My lords and gentlemen! The Court assembles.
Pray silence for the learned Commissioners . . .

A flourish of trumpets. All stand, and (preceded by MACERS, *with mace and sword, which they solemnly lay on the table), there enter* SIR PETER MALLORY, JOHN DE BACKWELL, *and* SIR RALPH DE SANDWICH, *as the* HERALD *cries their names.*

Sir Peter Mallory, Justiciar of England;
Master Justice John de Backwell; and Sir Ralph de Sandwich, Constable of the Tower of London.

*All that have places sit; and after a short pause, during which they
converse, there is a distant fanfare.*

My lords and gentlemen! Attend His Majesty,
The Lord Edward, King of England,
Lord of Ireland and Duke of Aquitaine!

All stand.

His Royal Highness Edward Prince of Wales!
His Grace the Archbishop of Canterbury, Primate of all
England,
The Lord Bishop of Chichester, Chancellor of England,
The Lord Thomas Earl of Lancaster, Steward of England.

Grand fanfare. Enter KING EDWARD *and the others, with atten-
dants.* EDWARD *seats himself on the throne.*

KING EDWARD

Pray be seated, my lords.

All sit.

Well, Mallory, all your evidence
Is assembled?

MALLORY [*pointing at documents on table*]
As you see, Majesty.

KING EDWARD

There seems plenty of it, certainly.
And your pen sharp?

MALLORY
As a sword, sire.

KING EDWARD [*laughing*]

Well, Mallory, well and good.
But you are only three. Three is a quorum,
Certies, but where are your fellows?

A burst of cheers and jeers, off. Church bells ring.

MALLORY

The mob answers for me, sire. Sir John
De Segrave and His Worship the Mayor
Lead the escort of the prisoner—

KING EDWARD

The dog—

MALLORY

The dog, Your Majesty.

Cheers and bells, off.

KING EDWARD

Yes, I had forgot the procession.
He has a considerable escort,
Constable, surely, for such a dog.

SANDWICH

Sire, the crowd is so great;
The whole of London is out.
He is a dangerous dog, but the mob
Is dangerous too, and we would preserve
Him yet awhile for justice' sake.
You could say, Your Majesty,
That we made him a public show
For his own protection.

KING EDWARD

Indeed, yes. I would not lose him now
After so much pains in getting him. Ha! Ha!

He laughs. Cheers, off.

PRINCE OF WALES

But those are cheers, surely, Constable!
Who in London could cheer such a rogue?
I would have the villains whipped.

SANDWICH

Doubtless they cheer His Worship the Mayor,
Highness, and the Sheriffs and Aldermen.
They would all go in the procession—

PRINCE OF WALES

Well, I would have them whipped anyway,
For their own good—

KING EDWARD

       As at Stirling, son?

PRINCE OF WALES

That was a year ago, my lord—
First tastes of pleasure sometimes shock
But grow sweet with habit—pain
Can give joy, humiliation ecstasy—
Whipping may be a kindness—

KING EDWARD

I never spared the rod.   You shall have
Your whips, Edward, by and by.
Now we have higher game.   But I like not
The delay.   Have our loyal Scots lords
Enter, herald, so they may welcome
Their hero becomingly.

HERALD

Sire.

Bows.   Trumpet flourish. SCOTS LORDS *enter as* HERALD *cries their names.*

My lords and gentlemen! Pray silence!
The Lords Bishops of Glasgow, St Andrews, and Dunkeld,
The Lord Robert, Earl of Huntingdon and Carrick,
The Earl of Ross, the Earl of Angus,
Sir Robert de Keith, Earl Marischal of Scotland,
Sir John de Mowbray, Sir John de Comyn, Sir John de
    Menteith [*murmurs in court* . . . .]

KING EDWARD

Welcome all, my lords and gentlemen.
Pray be seated. It is good to see you
Here, my Lord of Huntingdon.

BRUCE

Your Majestie.

KING EDWARD

        Loyal Menteith,
We are pleased indeed to have you with us
In the room of our true Blackbeard, Earl of March,
Who, unwisely as I think, begged leave
To indulge a fever. There is no lord
In Scotland merits more his place than you,
And no other was considered—for your interest.
We would have word with you in private
When this wretched business is despatched.
You will know that Edward is not niggardly
To those who have deserved his love.

MENTEITH

Your Majestie is kind, but nae reward
Can joy Menteith as this peace nou
That dawns at last for herried Scotland
And for England tae. Gif I hae my pairt
In this, I am content, and generations

143

Aye unborn sall bless my hand
That made them brithers that were mortal faes
And turned their bluidie brands til plousocks
In a nicht.   Yon's my reward, Majestie.

KING EDWARD

Most elevated sentiments, indeed, Sir John—
But never fear; you shall have more than that.
And, our other lords of Scotland,
We must thank you all who have accepted
Our gracious invitation—or obeyed
Our summons, shall we say?
It is perhaps unusual to see
So many Scottish lords and gentlemen
In an English court, but it was our wish
To have a chosen number of our most
Faithful and loyal subjects of Scotland
To see English justice done in an English
Court on a traitor to England's King.
Your presence makes our sorry business
So much more respectable—quite
A family affair, in fact, as Sir John
De Menteith might put it.   And besides,
None shall after have the right to say
That justice was not done.   You may
Always protest, sirs, if you see miscarriage.

*Murmurs in court.   Loud cheers, off.   Clatter of armed men, shouted
commands, etc.   Trumpet.*

Ah, I think our client arrives.

HERALD

Your Majesty, your Royal Highness,
Your Grace, my lords and gentlemen,
Pray silence for the Commissioners of Court:

Sir John de Segrave, Governor of Scotland,
And His Worship Sir John le Blunt,
Mayor of London, with the prisoner.

A hush.   Preceded by a STANDARD-BEARER *playing* sbandierata
*with the Bluidie Clout (which he sticks into a socket in the dock),
escorted by* BLUNT *and* SEGRAVE, *and guarded by four* GUARDS, *enter,
through audience,* WALLACE, *wearing a laurel crown, his clothes
ragged, his hands chained; and, hard at their heels, a rabble of
jeering* ENGLISH ARTISANS, APPRENTICES, *etc., who sit down on the
steps all round the stage.* SEGRAVE *and* BLUNT *bow to* KING
EDWARD, *and sit down.* WALLACE *does not bow.*

KING EDWARD

Kneel, dog!

WALLACE

I hae never kneel't yet.

A GUARD *strikes him, and he falls to his knees.*

KING EDWARD

You will now.

WALLACE

I kneel tae God; no til Edward.

KING EDWARD

Peace, wretch.   Put him in the dock. . . .

They put WALLACE *in the dock.*

We bid you welcome, Segrave,
My Lord Mayor.   You have guarded
Our prisoner well; he looks hale.
One request.   We would have a word
With the scoundrel before we deliver
Him over to the Court.   If that
Is in order, Justiciar?

MALLORY

Perfectly, Your Majesty.

KING EDWARD

                    Well, Wallace,
We've come a long way, you and I,
To this assize.   Eight years, I think,
It's been.   But the end is hardly
As you imagined it, I suppose.
Are you happy that we meet at last?

WALLACE

I never wished to meet ye, sir.
We were content wi our ain.   It was you
That cam til us, gin ye mynd?
But no by invitation.

KING EDWARD

                    Au contraire, messire.
The lords of Scotland invited me
Expressly to choose a king for them.

WALLACE

To choose, but no to rule.

KING EDWARD

It was my right.   But it was not you
I chose, Wallace, though I see you crowned
Before me now.   It becomes you well,
Base rogue.

WALLACE

I didna choose it.

My information tells me otherwise:
That you have boasted you should wear a crown
In Westminster Hall.   Well, you have your crown.
And I see you have a standard, too,
Like a real king.   What is that rag?   You will
Hardly need it now, at all events.
Give it me!

WALLACE

This, King Edward, like the croun,
They put on me for mockerie.   But

A GUARD *takes the Bluidie Clout to* EDWARD.

It isna me they mock.   The rag ye haud
In your hands is a rag o' bluid—
A woman's bluid spilt by an English man
Ye set in authoritie owre us.
I swore to revenge yon bluid,
And weill revengit it has been.
It's come hame t'ye at the last
And it isna me it mocks.

KING EDWARD

Poh!   That's what
I think of your blood and your rag and your
Mockery, slave!

He rives the flag in half, and flings it from him.

What right have you
To a banner?   What right have you to bear
Arms against your sovereign and anointed
Overlord?   Answer me, dog!

WALLACE

I am
Nae dug, sir, and I never anointit ye.

                                        Wretch,
Do you arrogate to yourself all grace?
Is there no limit to your presumption?
Who called on you to raise your banners
Against the might of Edward?

                    WALLACE
                        My folk.

                    KING EDWARD

Your folk?   Your natural lords—see them!—
Admit me as overlord and superior
And arbiter of their kingdom.   Who are
You, a younger son of a petty knight,
To deny me authority?

                    WALLACE
                    A kintra
Is its folk, sir, mair nor its lords.

                    KING EDWARD

A country is no country without a king.

                    WALLACE

Your Majestie is mistaken.   And we
Had a king, and sall hae anither.

    BRUCE *lifts his head sharply, and* COMYN *looks at him.*

                    KING EDWARD

There you are right, Wallace.   You have one now
And you look upon him.   We meet at last,
Face to face.   I could wish it had been
In happier circumstances.   We could have

Worked together, Wallace, had you wished.
You have great qualities—this I respect.
Had you wished, I could have helped them fructify.
You are a man of power, Wallace.

WALLACE *raises his chained arms.*

Your chains could be stricken off
At a word. Forgive me, these precautions
Are necessary on occasion,
But I am a merciful man to those
Who do not thwart me. They were not
My orders that had you chained
And barefoot on your journey here.
It has certainly been a very hot summer.
I repeat, I had the power
To help you, had you chosen right.

WALLACE

Edward had the pouer to help, but Edward
Didna order the chains or gar the sun
Burn in the heat o' the day. Edward
Didna lowse the chains nae mair nor Edward
Summoned the clouds o' flees and clegs
And the stour on the rubble roads o' England
In midsimmer, ruggit at the tail o' a mear,
Barefuit, bareheidit, waterless.
Edward didna order the public shawin
O' the rebel Wallace in ilka toun
On the road. Edward wantit Wallace
Alive, and Edward has me alive,
And yon's the stent of Edward's pouer.
I am here to pruve King Edward's pouer,
And the blacken't villages o' Scotland
Tell the like potent tale. But maybe
The stent o' the pouer's diminished a wee
When ye think it took the micht o' Edward's

149

Feudal chivalrie nae less nor echt lang year
And sax invasions o' a peacefu land
To kep a single man—and failed, at that—
To win at last by foulest traitorie.
Maybe the pouer to help is no sae muckle
As it seems gin the pouer to hurt's
Sae poverisht—

KING EDWARD

Be still, dog!
You've said enough.   You are not here
To preach at us in our own court.

WALLACE

Edward can steek my mou wi a word
But truth he canna ding—it will speak on
When he and I are dust and never will
Be silenced.

KING EDWARD

Your time is near, Wallace.

WALLACE

And yours, Majestie.   Flesh is grass.
A peerie space divides us nou,
But for your sons' sons and mine,
And their sons' sons, we are thegither aye.
Centuries and generations
Canna twyne us.   We are bunden in
Aefauld embrace like bride and groom
In ae strauchle indivisible—
I in triumphand daith, and you
In fructless victorie.

KING EDWARD

Silence, I say!
Rogue, I'll not submit to this—

But ye dae! Ye ken the truth o't, conqueror!
My chains pleisure me nae mair nor you
Your victorie—they gall me as muckle
As your guilt does you. I can lowse
Mine nae mair nor you can yours.
Sir, we maun thole us baith our agonies.

KING EDWARD

Suffering has made you philosophical
As well as impertinent, slave.
But I would not have you share your maudlin
Consolations with me. Know, Wallace,
That you stand before me in defeat.
Look round and you will see some known faces
Who took the wiser course and made their peace.
I said I could be generous to those
Who did not thwart me. Those who do must feel
The full weight of a power that no
Philosophy will lighten by so much
As a feather's load. You are right—
It has taken me eight years to have you
Here before me, eight years to subjugate
The rebelliousness of your savage race
Against their rightful King—

WALLACE

                    Edward will ne'er
Be King o' Scots for all his vaunting.

KING EDWARD

Be silent, thief! I tell you when to speak,
As I tell your countrymen when to come
And go. My displeasure rises,
And that will prove the worse for you. Be wise.

Scotland I have conquered. Look around.
I have fought many wars, Wallace;
More than you have or ever will;
In the Holy Land, in Gascony,
In Wales; and everywhere God has blessed
My arms. Is that not enough for you?
But no war, no conquest I have made
In a man's lifetime of wars, has warmed
My blood as it rejoices now. Scotland
By her frowartness, her stupid
Ignorance of where her profits lie,
Has angered me as no other has.
I would liefer far be lord of Scotland
Than Seigneur of France or Spain,
Or even the vast territories
Of the Infidel. Wallace, would you hear
A secret?

WALLACE

  I hae nae pouer to wish
Or to unwish.

KING EDWARD

  As you have reminded me,
I am old. Soon I shall die, and die happy.
With Scotland unsubdued this could not be,
But God has blessed my arms, right has prevailed,
And I would wish all future Kings of England
To know this. I shall die, Wallace, yes,
And on my tomb I wish no more remembrance
Than for this. Four words I've ordered to be cut
—No more, my proudest boast, my immortality:
"EDWARDUS PRIMUS, MALLEUS SCOTORUM":
"Edward the First, Hammer of the Scots."
And you too will be remembered in those words.
Your fate will be my proof. You are honoured
In dishonour, Wallace.

Sir, you honour
Me far mair nor yet ye dream of.

KING EDWARD

That was gracefully said.   But now
Let us hear more of Wallace.   He had
A bad journey in the sun, he says—

WALLACE

I bear nae malice, sir.   Juist skaiths.

KING EDWARD

Wallace can inflict " skaiths " too.
You have heard my epitaph.   Would it give
You pleasure to hear yours?

WALLACE

I'll hae nae lair,
Nor stane to scart memorial on.

KING EDWARD

There you speak truth.   But your deeds will have
Memorial, wretch—as you will see.
It is not for me, however, to usurp
The duties of the Court.   Sir John
De Segrave, I return you your prisoner.
Justiciar, pray proceed.   Wallace
And my loyal Scottish lords, hearken
To a rebel's epitaph.   By the looks
Of things it will be somewhat longer
Than a king's.   *Fiat justitia!*

Your Majesty's servant. [*Banging his gavel*] The Court
Is in session. Sir Geoffrey de Hartlepool,
Messire Recorder, will you rehearse
The indictment of the prisoner at the bar,
The rebel and traitor William le Wallace.

HARTLEPOOL [*reading from parchment*]

My lords, the accused, William le Wallace, a native of Scotland,
is in this Court indicted of the foul crimes of treason, sedition,
rebellion, murder, robbery, arson, sacrilege, and sundry other
felonies. My lords, after our lord Edward, the King, had made
conquest of Scotland and had brought all Scots into submission
and subjugation to his royal dominion and power, and when,
as their King, he had publicly received the homages and fealties
of all prelates, earls, barons, and others of Scotland and had
caused his peace to be proclaimed throughout the land, and had
appointed governors, sheriffs, and other officers to maintain
that peace and to do justice, then it was that the accused
William the Wallace, abrogating his allegiance to the King, did
traitorously and seditiously make insurrection against him, together with a confederacy of other vast numbers of felons, and
did feloniously invade and attack the governors and ministers
of the King, and especially did attack and slay and cut into
pieces William de Heselrig, Sheriff of Lanark, and with a
multitude of armed men did invade the towns, cities and castles
of that country, and did send forth his writs throughout the
whole of Scotland as the overlord of that country, and did also
hold parliaments and assemblies without right, and did expel
the governors and officers of his rightful King. *Further,* with
other felons, he did invade the English counties of Northumber-
land, Cumberland and Westmoreland, and did wickedly slay
all there that he found loyal to the King, not excluding priests
and nuns of God. There also did he destroy churches built to
the honour of God and His saints, disturbed the bodies of the

saints and also did cast down, burn and devastate these holy buildings and their relics, and with more barbarity than can be conceived did put to death all whom he met, old men and young, wives and widows, children and sucklings. *Furthermore*, without cease, every day and every hour, this traitor William did treasonably plot the death of his King and the destruction of his authority and royal dignity. Even after the King with a great army had overthrown the accused, and had mercifully offered him to come into his peace, the said traitor William still wickedly and treasonably refused to submit himself. Accordingly, by the laws and customs of England and Scotland, the accused was outlawed as traitor, robber and felon, was taken captive by loyal servants of the King and is here arraigned as guilty of treason, murder, rebellion, sacrilege, and other unspeakable crimes already listed in the preamble [*murmurs in court*]. *Finally*, as it is unjust and contrary to the laws of England that any outlaw can plead protection of the law or speak in accusation or defence in any court of law unless he be first restored to the King's peace, and whereas the accused has stubbornly refused the merciful clemency of the King in offering him that restoration to grace, it is here averred that the said William has no right here to plead in his own defence and that accordingly sentence should be passed instanter and forthwith.

Court murmur. Trumpet. MALLORY *rises to pronounce doom.* EDWARD *motions him to desist.*

KING EDWARD

Uncustomary though it be, we have
A small request, Justiciar.
We should like to hear the accused—
Unrestored outlaw though he be—
If the Court will be indulgent.
Our loyal Scottish lords must have no
Complaint of English justice. Sir Peter?

Sire, this is Your Majesty's own court.

KING EDWARD [*without anger*]
Traitor, rebel, vandal, murderer,
What have you to say?

WALLACE
I never was a traitor, Edward.

KING EDWARD
You have heard the indictment.

WALLACE
I was never liege of Edward,
I was never traitor to my King.

KING EDWARD
I am your King, you are my liege.

WALLACE
The King of Scots was my King.

KING EDWARD
I am the King of Scots now, Wallace.

WALLACE
No, sir. Yon's a dream ye had.
Ye'll wauken frae it in a wee.

KING EDWARD
I know of no other King of Scots.

WALLACE

Whase faut is yon?

KING EDWARD

That is not decorous in this place.

WALLACE

I didna choose the place, sir.
In Scotland decorum isna expeckit
Or requirit in an outlaw.

KING EDWARD

You are in England now, Wallace.

WALLACE [*with a glance at the* SCOTS LORDS]
Forgie me, Majestie. I had forgot.

SCOTS LORDS *stir and girn and look uneasy.*

KING EDWARD

You are a brave man, Wallace, and I can
Respect a warrior; even, perhaps,
In the balance, forgive him his
Barbarities.   You have given me
A thought, just now.

WALLACE

They are nae bonnie thochts
That I can gie, Majestie.

KING EDWARD

You may jest. But hearken to me.
You have done me great wrong, assuredly,
As you have heard at some length.
None of this you deny.

157

WALLACE

I deny treason.

KING EDWARD

Well, let us leave that by the way for now.
I can respect your loyalty too, Wallace.
I would win it.

WALLACE

It's no for winnin,
Edward, or for sale.

KING EDWARD

The war is over now,
Wallace, finished for ever.

WALLACE

For the saxt time in echt year—

KING EDWARD

For the last time; for at last I have you.
We need never fight again, our peoples.
We can be brothers, as Menteith has said—

WALLACE

Doesna your thrapple boke to speak
The name? Commend me til the rats
And puddocks as wyce men afore ye cry on that—

MENTEITH [*upstanding*]

Sire, I protest! Maun I thole this felon's
Flyting without let? Has leal Menteith
In Edward's court nae shield agane a traitor?

WALLACE

The Deil quotes Scripture couthilie—

KING EDWARD

Silence! I'll have no Scotch bickers in my court!
Rebel, you speak when called upon.
Sir John, I'm sure you can protect yourself
As well as I from the idle taunts
Of a captive. You wish to address him?

MENTEITH

I wish to silence him.

WALLACE

Time winna silence the chitterin shame
Upon ye, Menteith. Hide your face!

MENTEITH

I hae nae shame, Wallace, and I dinna fear
The verdict of time. The future
Is wi me, no you. You are the past,
Tho bad auld past of bluid and fear and enmitie
That dees wi you in this court the day.
The future is mine, wi peace
And comitie atween twa realms; the haill
Land o' Britain acfauld under ae king, ae law;
Enemies nae mair but friends and brithers.
Yon's what time will say. And say for me—no you.

WALLACE

Ye're sae strang on the days to come, Menteith,
In luve and comitie wi your maister here,
Ye've forgot we were peacefu eneuch afore
He ever cam to woo us—sword in hand.
There was nae bluid till Edward spilt it;
There's be nae peace till Scot and Sudron
Speaks as equals man to man. What man
That's a man speaks peace wi a dirk at his craig?

Or wad ye gie the wolf to keep the wedder?
Gin the lion speak peace til the lamb
He maunna eat the lamb—!

KING EDWARD

Wallace a lamb! Ho! Ho! But, still. . . .
Menteith you cannot love, but Menteith is right.

MENTEITH *sits*.

England and Scotland could thrive at peace
If the Scots wish—

WALLACE
Gif the English—

KING EDWARD [*reasonably*]
No, be still and hear me out.

WALLACE

I can nocht ither, sire.

KING EDWARD

Now that we are at peace, I can afford
To be merciful—ask your countrymen!

The SCOTS LORDS *fidget*.

Even wise—though that is more difficult.
I said, " If the Scots wish it,"—I did not
Mean " If the Scots cease to harry England,"
But " If the Scots will be at peace with one
Another." You have given me a notion
That could heal the wounds of Scotland's enmities.
Scotland is vanquished, Scotland is subject,
But Scotland must be ruled. Who will do it?
An English viceroy but provokes their blood—

As you have reminded us, Wallace.
For true peace, Scotland must not be
Subordinate. *Ergo,* I must rule Scotland
With a Scot. But who?

    The SCOTS LORDS *stir and murmur.*

You have two great families opposed,
Bruce and Comyn. My lords, if I favour
One of you, I make an enemy
Of tother—and I have war. Now we have peace
And all good men wish to keep it so.
I cannot choose you both to rule—
I will choose neither.

Uproar among the SCOTS LORDS. BRUCE *and* COMYN *start up.*

          BRUCE

Your Majestie—!

          COMYN
    Never will I—!

    MALLORY *bangs his gavel.*

      KING EDWARD

My lords, this is not seemly!

    They murmur but subside.

Pray restrain yourselves and hear your King.
You have guessed my thoughts, I see.
I know you have no love for the prisoner;
Your rank was envious of his power—
It is not envious now, I think.
Wallace, I shall remedy all this.
I shall create a dukedom for you.
A dignity and elevation above
All Scottish, yea, all English, rank. As Duke
Of Scotland you shall be my Viceroy

Beyond Tweed, with lands sufficient
To your title and power to hold
Your precedence beyond the reach of any
Combination in the land. Owing liege
To none but me, you will rule Scotland
Wisely, strongly, peaceably, and safely.
You have the quality; I can give you
Might to marry it. Scotland will be
Great and England grateful.

Pause.

Well?

WALLACE

Certies, there's some thocht I've gied ye, Majestie:
Certies, there's some richt in what ye say:
Certies, I hae ruled ere this and could again,
And maybe, wi God's help, could hale
The enmities sae rank amang the rank
O' Scotland . . .

Murmurs.

Ay.

Pause.

Deed ay.

Pause.

A thocht it is.
And a braw thing in truth to hae the land at peace
That trauchles wearie wi the lang skaith of war—

KING EDWARD [*sincerely*]

Both lands, Wallace. My thought
Is mutual benefit for us both.
I said I could be generous: I mean to all.
No harm I see, but only good, can breed
From such a contract—

WALLACE

Ay, Majestie, ye hae a thocht, indeed.
Great pouer in my grip and pouer for guid. . . .
Yon's a temptacious thocht for onie man. . . .
And efter sae lang a feud—

KING EDWARD

You may have time to think upon't.

Pause.

WALLACE

Juist so. . . .

Pause.

Juist so.—Or a tempter's, maybe?
Ah, Edward, tell me this: Wad ye gie me
Menteith for my Chancellor?

MENTEITH

Your Majestie!

KING EDWARD

A moment, Sir John.
You are pleased to jest, Wallace—

WALLACE

How, sir?
What mair likelier or mair fitter
Doer than Menteith for Wallace, Edward's
Duke of Scotland? Na, Majestie, methinks
It wasna me gied ye the thocht, but his sel.
Mak him your pluckit duke, why no?

KING EDWARD

Menteith is not the subject of debate,
But Wallace. I ask you not to jest.

I dinna jest, Majestie.

Is this your answer, then?

Nane ither.

I cannot understand you.
This is not the wisdom I'd expect from
Such an adversary.   And yet you are not mad
—Or seem not so.   Can it be that pride,
That vanity, that was your final downfall?
That refused, for arrogance and grandeur,
To bow to greater men in your degree
And at last presumed even to a crown . . . ?

I hae my croun, Majestie.

[*laughing*]
You have indeed, Wallace!
Alas for pride that goes before a fall!
It is not Scotland's nor yet England's—
Ah!   I see!—and so you grasp, poor upstart,
In despair, for one of martyrdom!
This is the very meridian of vanity!
You should be content with your laurels, surely,
Though they be no conqueror's—Indeed,

He laughs.

They may become a martyr's, after all!
But now I offer you a nobler crest,

164

The first under the Crown of Scotland.
Is this not vanity's reward enough?
But, seriously. Think again. I assure you
I would not regret it. Be my Duke, Wallace!

WALLACE

Regrets there'd be aaricht! And gin
They werena yours, Edward, then certies
They'd be mine! And I assure you, sir,
In earnest, tae, Menteith wad suit ye better.
Ye'd understand him fine. Ay, he's your man.

KING EDWARD

Enough of Menteith, I say!
How can you refuse?

WALLACE

Honour refuses.

KING EDWARD

Honour! What honour? Of a rebel,
Vandal, murderer?

WALLACE

Of a man!
And of a Scottish man!

KING EDWARD

Of a fool,
And of a blind ingrate fool!

WALLACE

Gin a Scottish man was gratefu
For aa the mercies of Edward,
Ay, he'd be a fule indeed—and blind.

You speak of Edward's mercy with a mock—
I'll not be angered.   But, I ask, what king
Has ever offered, after treason,
Such magnanimity to a foe prostrate?
Or such elevation?   How can you
Refuse?

WALLACE

How can I nocht?
I never was a traitor, Edward.

KING EDWARD [*flying up*]

What do you mean?
Why do you repeat this rote?   It becomes
Meaningless.   Do you not see where fortune
Beckons and greatness lies?   Traitor to whom?
As Duke of Scotland how can you be traitor
To Scotland?   You will not be traitor to me.

WALLACE

Then sall I be traitor to Scotland.
Edward, ye speak of greatness,
Ye speak of elevation, title, and the lave—
D'ye no see, as I said, ye've elevatit
Me eneuch or this.   I wish
Nae further glorie than ye've gied me here.
I winna be your Duke.   I'm content wi this.
This is my elevation and my granderie.

KING EDWARD [*laughing*]

Ah, noble Wallace!

WALLACE

Ay, noble!   And wha made me noble, sir?
Ye cried me vauntie, fule, and ingrate.   Fule

And vauntie, maybe ay, but trulie grateful, Edward.
Maybe in this they aa three gang thegither.
Wad I hae my laurel croun gin you'd
Never lustit efter Scotland's?
Gin ye'd never socht to thirl a freeborn
Folk of aulder race nor England's?
This croun, I say, mocks you, no me.
When ye said I wished to wear a croun
In England, ye but faithered your ain thocht
On me. I never wish't a croun, and certies,
No a croun of martyrdom. I dinna wish
It nou; I feel it like a ring o' fire
On my brou, but I rejoice that ye hae
Liftit me sae hiech abune the princes
And the tyrants o' the yerth—yon
Is my boast, and yon my vaunitie!

KING EDWARD

You are avid of the fire, Wallace;
Beware your prophecy prove too true.
Pride is easily humbled, fool! Pain
Is a great leveller, and agony
Unmans a man. Be warned.

WALLACE

Princes
Are loftit owre the common ruck,
The een o' the world is on them.
They should be princelie, sire. When they
Bemean lesser men they but bemean
Theirsels. It wasna Oliphant humiliate
At Stirling Siege, but Edward.
Nae Edward has his triumph here,
Nor yet his scullion Menteith, but Wallace,
Ay, and Scotland—for ye've jynit
Thae twa names thegither in aa times to come.

This is nocht the daith of Wallace, Edward,
Nor yet the end of Scotland, in your
Menteith-peace, or desert-conquest either,
But the birth-thraws of its glorie and its
Triumph. Scotland has wan, my lord, and you,
Nane ither, gied us victorie. . . .

KING EDWARD

Ha!

Murmurs.

WALLACE

Through this lang war, echt year o' fire and sword
And famine, greit and bluid and daith,
Ye've made a nation, sir. Hammer
O' the Scots indeed! By the Rood,
Ye're richter nor ye ken. Ye've hammerit
A nation intil life, ennobled it,
And held it up like a banner til aa men
For evermair—a standart o' the pride
And independence of a folk whase sperit's
Free and winna bou til thirldom ever—
No for land or treisure, consequence
Or pouer, but for ae thing that, wanting,
Leas life wersh and thowless, dozent,
Meaningless; but, possess't, lets man stand
Upricht in the likeness of his God
That made him sae: Freedom! Ay, thirldom
Is the soul in chains—e'en in the mid o' plentie,
As libertie is the soul at lairge—though
It be in puirtith and defeat. This we hae wan.
For aa this, Edward, I, in the name o' Scotland,
First o' the nations, thank ye, for your gift
Til aa humanitie. *You* should be vauntie,
Sir! Put aff yon dowie look! Your

168

Immortalitie is in sauf keep, juist
As ye said, SCOTORUM MALLEUS—

Murmurs.

KING EDWARD

It is dangerous to mock a king,
You and your so-called nation—what is that?
You have great eloquence, rebel,
And greater insolence. For my part
I have had great patience, which is now
Exhausted quite. Also, you rebuke
My generosity, and that touches
My pride where it is vulnerable.
You have rejected the mace of power, fool—
You shall feel the weight of the hammer.
Are you prepared for judgment?

WALLACE

Ay, and readie, Majestie. I hae my croun.
Men say the martyrs gaed til the arena
And the fire wi hymns o' joy. Sae gang I
Til your scaffold. Nay, mair, like them
I'll prophesie. Scotland has wan, I say,
And sae ye'll see, or a twalmonth's out,
A king, and no an English king, sall sit
In Scone, and Edward tak the wearie road
Again and get nae victorie again,
Nor ever will—it is owre late—

KING EDWARD

Thou hast said! Enough, enough! I'll no more
Of this! The churl begins to rave
Like a saint indeed. His wits are out.
And you forget, witless,
In your prophecies, that other

Rune that tells that he who sits upon
The Stone of Scone shall rule the Scots.
I sit upon it here and now, fool.
I am your King.

WALLACE [*laughing*]
            The Stane ye hae
Is no the richt Stane, as weill ye ken.
And the rune ye speak isna the richt ane,
Either—as again ye ken fu weill:
It says the Scots sall rule whar the Stane is!—
Your Latin is as guid as mine. . . .

KING EDWARD

So the villain now turns scholar, eh? Ha!
You over-reach yourself, my learned clown.
And I have indulged you over-long.
You weary me. The audience is ended.
Now we shall demonstrate the " ruling "
Of the Scots, *pardie!* Justiciar, to judgment,
Sparing nothing! And you to your prayers,
Traitor! See how high I raise you now!

Flourish of trumpets.

MALLORY [*reading from parchment*]

It has been adjudged by the Commissioners of the King's
Court of Justiciary sitting in Westminster Great Hall this
twenty-third day of August, Monday in the Vigils of Saint
Bartholomew, in the thirty-third year of his reign, that the
accused rebel and traitor William the Wallace, for his manifest
sedition and treason against his sovereign lord the King, for
his wicked machinations in plotting the King's death and bear-
ing banner against his liege lord, shall be led from the Palace of
Westminster to the Tower of London, and from the Tower to
Aldgate, and so through the midst of the City to the Elms of
Smithfield, and there, for the robberies, murders, and felonies

committed in the realm of England and the land of Scotland, he shall be hanged by the neck, and let down half-living, and his parts of manhood cut off, and, for the vast injuries done to God and Holy Church, that his heart, liver, lungs, and all his inner parts whereout such abominable and perverse imaginations proceeded, shall be drawn and cast into a fire and burnt before his face, and, because he be an outlaw, unrestored, despite repeated invitations, to the King's grace, that he shall be beheaded; and also. . . .

All through this, there has been much murmuring among the SCOTS LORDS, *and now* BRUCE *springs to his feet, while his neighbours try to restrain him.*

BRUCE

No! No! Sire, your Majestie! No!
I beg ye! Sic ferocitie o' sentence
Is luxurious!

KING EDWARD [*thundering*]
My lord of Carrick!

BRUCE

No! Rebel or nae rebel, Wallace
Is a man and warrior of honour!
Hae his heid, gin ye will, the axe
Is honourable. But no, I beg ye,
No this bluid-shotten butcherie!
This is ignominie! And no to be
Tholit! 'Tis ower dour! I canna
Thole it! And I shall nocht thole it!

He struggles from his place on to the floor of the Court.

Ah! Bruce's road is plain at last—
Wallace, ye win indeed! I winna
Thole it, Edward! Mark me weill—and there's

He flings down his gauntlet.

171

My gage upon't to cairrie wi ye
Intae Scotland aince again—
You or your shilpit brat!

He breenges out through the crowd of LORDS, OFFICIALS, *and*
SOLDIERS, *who are momentarily afraid to lay hands on him.*

KING EDWARD [*on his feet*]

Arrest Lord Carrick!
Seize him! Guards! To arms!

Trumpets, off. Too late, GUARDS *take action.*

Bruce must not leave London!
Segrave, after him! Why do you stand?
Ride all night! He must be taken!

SEGRAVE *runs out with other* ENGLISH LORDS.

Hurry, hurry, hurry! He will be away!

EDWARD *sinks back on his throne. He is old and trembling. The*
PRINCE OF WALES *has his face in his hands.*

WALLACE

Ay, he'll be weill awa, Edward!
He was richt, tae. I hae wan. I hae kent it
Echt lang year, and nou it's true.
Ay, I've wan indeed!

EDWARD *rises in a passion, slaps* WALLACE *on both his cheeks,
snatches off his laurel crown, and rives it in bits. It falls beside the
Bluidie Clout.*

KING EDWARD

Ah, dog! Dog! Take him away! This must end!
Wallace alive, I know no peace,
Now he has lost me Bruce! Take him away!

WALLACE [*laughing*]

Owre late, Majestie, owre late!

Trumpets. WALLACE *is surrounded by* GUARDS.

WALLACE [*to* SCOTS LORDS]

Fareweill, my lords. This is nocht the end—
Edward—

He is hustled out.

Scotland . . . !

KING EDWARD [*hands to lugs, screaming*]

Take him away! He must die! And quickly!
No, no! Let it be slow, very slow,
And beautiful. . . .

Trumpets. All LORDS *in uproar.* WALLACE *is led out. Clash of
weapons. All this while, the Court is still in session, and* MALLORY
is reading, albeit inaudibly, the dooming.

MALLORY

. . . And also, because of his foresaid manifold enormities,
seditions and other felonies, that the body of the said William
shall be cut and divided in four quarters and the head be set
on the Bridge of London in sight of all passing by land and
water. One quarter of the body shall be hung on the gallows
at Newcastle-upon-Tyne, over the common sewers, another
quarter at Berwick, a third quarter at Perth, and the fourth
quarter of his body on the gates of Stirling for the dread and
chastisement of all that pass and behold them.

Heavy doors clang. Trumpets. Mob cheers.

The SCOTS LORDS—*all save* MENTEITH, *who, head high, walks
swiftly out—bow their heads, and, still bowed, not looking at each
other, turn their backs, and slowly, not together, but singly, go out.*

KING EDWARD

Now I must start all over again . . . Menteith!

But MENTEITH *is through the door.*

Comyn, a word with you.

COMYN

It has been said, my lord.

Pause.

But no by me.

Pause.

And no by you.

COMYN *turns his back and exit slowly. The court clears in silence.* KING EDWARD *staggers to his throne and sits alone, exhausted, brooding.*

KING EDWARD [*muttering*]

What did he mean?

Pause. Distant cries of " Wallace! Wallace! " Lights dim slowly, one spot remaining on the fragments of the Bluidie Clout and the laurel crown. KING EDWARD *rises, walks slowly to pick up the Clout, and stands, looking at it in his hands, in complete silence.*

KING EDWARD [*scornfully, desperately*]

Wallace!

Pause. Lights dimming. Distant trumpet. Lights dim out. Long pause in darkness.

Lights up. To a slowly-mounting crescendo of drums, the whole cast re-enters and assembles on stage. Then, finally, with a great crash, the orchestra breaks into the air " Scots wha hae wi Wallace bled."

FINIS

APPENDIX

THREE SONGS

POSTSCRIPTUM

THREE SONGS

I. *Soldiers' Song, for the Beginning of Act II: above, p. 47*

Hey, King Edward wi the lang shanks,
Berwick ye've taen withouten thanks,
By and by ye'll get your paiks
    Wi " Up, lads, and pike him! "
And when he's doun,
" Up, lads, and dyke him! "

II. *Another, for the Same*

Syne sweet Annot did me say
We'll meet again anither day
    Wi a hoolie, hoolie, rumble-de-O!
    Wi a hoolie, rumble-de-O,
      My hinnie,
    A hoolie rumble-de-O!

Gentle butler, bellamy,
Fill the bottle by the eye
That we may drink till by and by
    With " Ho, butler, ho! "
    Fill the bottle, butler,
    And let the cup roll!

I am so dry I cannot speak,
I am nigh chokéd with my meat,
I trow the butler be asleep—
    With " Ho, butler, ho! "
    Fill the bottle, butler,
    And let the cup roll!

POSTSCRIPTUM

Auctorial Note for Pedants

The historical materials for this period in Scotland are scant; and traditional or legendary material can never be discounted altogether. One of Blind Harry's "wild romances"—Wallace's visit to France—was shown to be right in the nineteenth century, four hundred years after Harry sang, by a document found in the Tower of London.

A deal of the documentary matter has been brought together by Joseph Stevenson in *Documents Illustrative of Sir William Wallace* (Maitland Club, 1841); and the epic poem of *Wallace* by Henry the Minstrel (Blind Harry) is the great storehouse of the popular tales as courant in Scotland a century and a half after the hero's death.

I would point out some instants of poetic licence in the play to save the learned from the fash of bringing them to my notice.

Act I. By tradition, Wallace's wife was slain by the Sheriff of Lanark, or at his command, for helping Wallace escape through her house when pursued by the English (Wyntoun, *c.* 1418). All we know for certain is that Wallace took his revenge on "Willelmum de Heselregg, vicecomitem de Lanarke"—for this is specifically cited in his indictment, along with his "aliis diversis feloniis."

Act II. Harry has Bruce and Wallace in argument from opposite banks of the Carron Water after Falkirk. History is no help here and I see no reason why they should not have thrashed things out before the battle—as well as, or better than after.

Act III. I have antedated the freeing of Haliburton by some months.

Act IV. There is no historical reference to Ailish Rae as such. In the Arundel MS, we learn that Wallace was betrayed in the house of one Rauf Raa, near Glasgow. By Harry's time the steading had become " Rob Ra's toun " (farm); it is now Robroyston, a suburb of Glasgow. De Brunne's Chronicle tells us that Menteith took Wallace " when he weened least, on nyght, his leman by." I have given her a name.

Act V. One chronicler of Wallace's end (in the Royal MS) tells that Edward would not confront his enemy (" ne le voleit regarder "), but three others, all English, tell that Wallace did indeed come before the King,[1] and one of the three, Matthew of Westminster, adds even that the King himself wished to sit in judgment—" volente rege de ipso fieri judicium." The other five or six documents are silent on the question, one way or the other.

Scots lords being present at the trial has no documentary warrant, but the possibility cannot be thrown out when we consider that, just three weeks later, a Parliament with ten Scottish commissioners (including Menteith as substitute for Patrick Earl of March) convened at Westminster to settle the future governance of Scotland. Bruce had been present at Westminster for the Lent Parliament, five months before, and had been one of Edward's advisers who had picked the names of these ten Scottish commissioners. Seven months after Wallace's execution, having slain the Reid Comyn, Bruce was crowned King of Scots at Scone.

S. G. S.

---

[1] *Scalacronica:* "(fust) amienez au roy Dengleterre qi ly fist treiner & pendre." *Lanercost:* " . . . ad regem adductus et adjudicatus fuit."